SOUTH WEST COAST PATH

Padstow to Falmouth

D1514162

NATIONAL TRAIL GUIDES

SOUTH WEST COAST PATH

Padstow to Falmouth

John Macadam

Photographs by Mike Williams

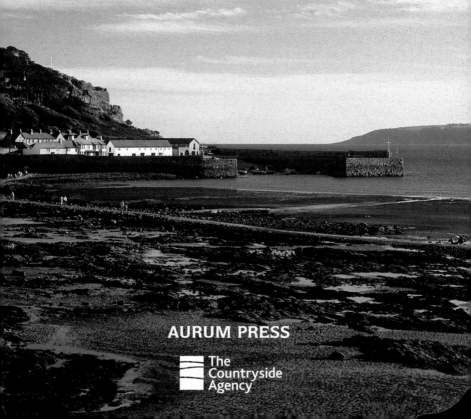

AURUM PRESS

The
Countryside
Agency

ACKNOWLEDGEMENTS

My thanks go to everyone who commented on the first edition: the remaining inadequacies are mine. My special thanks go to Nick Johnson of the Cornwall Archaeological Unit; Roger Radcliffe of the St Agnes Museum Trust; Lyn Jenkins and Ray Lawman of the Nature Conservancy Council now English Nature; Charlie David and Tim Dingle of the North Cornwall Heritage Coast Service; Steve Hall; Dave Lewis and Steve Scoffin, countryside rangers; Brian Coombes; Malcolm McCarthy; Peter Hall; Ralph Bird; Robin Meneer; Frank Middleditch; Bill Newby; Sophie Boumahdi; Clive Carter; Jean McCubbin; Nigel and Jane Haward; Joan and the late Roy Davis; the ever-patient and helpful staff at Bodmin Library; the Cove Inn at Cadgwith; the South West Way Association; and many people working for the National Trust and the county and district councils in Cornwall, particularly Richard Horwood and the Coast Path wardens, Malcolm Drover and Roger Parrott, who keep the path in good shape for walkers. Finally my thanks go to Helen and Frances for running a taxi service and for testing some of the circular walks, too.

John Macadam was brought up in Devon, and has been using the Coast Path since 1965. Since 1972 he has lived in Cornwall, working as a lecturer, writer and guide. He is chairman of the geological conservation group of the Cornwall Wildlife Trust, and a member of the Outdoor Writers' Guild.

John Dehane Macadam has asserted his rights under Section 77 of the Copyright, Designs and Patents Act 1988 to be identified as the author of this work.

This guide has been compiled in accordance with the Guidelines for Writers of Path Guides published by the Outdoor Writers' Guild.

This revised edition first published 2000 by Aurum Press Ltd in association with the Countryside Agency

Text copyright © 1990, 1996, 2000 by Aurum Press Ltd and the Countryside Agency
Maps Crown copyright © 1990, 1996, 2000 by the Ordnance Survey
Photographs copyright © 1990, 1996 by the Countryside Agency

Ordnance Survey and Pathfinder are registered trademarks and the OS symbol, Outdoor Leisure and Explorer are trademarks of Ordnance Survey, the National Mapping Agency of Great Britain.

A catalogue record for this book is available from the British Library

ISBN 1 85410 673 2
1 3 5 4 2
2000   2002   2003   2001

Book design by Robert Updegraff
Cover photograph: Lautivet Bay
Title page photograph: St Michael's Mount

Typset by Wyvern Typesetting Ltd, Bristol
Printed and bound in Italy by Printer Srl, Trento

CONTENTS

Circular walks appear on pages 26, 48, 61, 86 and 106

How to use this guide

The 613-mile (987-kilometre) South West Coast Path is covered by four national trail guides. This book describes the Coast Path from Padstow to Falmouth, 164 miles (264 kilometres). Companion guides describe the Coast Path from Minehead to Padstow, from Falmouth to Exmouth, and from Exmouth to Poole. Each guide therefore covers a section of the Coast Path between major estuaries, where walkers may need a ferry or other transport.

This guide is in three parts:

• The introduction, historical background to the area and advice for walkers.

• The Coast Path itself, described in thirteen chapters, with maps opposite each route description. This part of the guide also includes information on places of interest as well as a number of related short walks, either starting from the path itself or at a car park. Key sites are numbered in the text and on the maps to make it easy to follow the route description.

• The last part includes useful information, such as local transport, ferries and river crossings, accommodation, organisations involved with the Coast Path, and further reading.

The maps have been prepared by the Ordnance Survey® using 1:25000 Pathfinder®, Explorer™ or Outdoor Leisure™ maps as a base. The line of the Coast Path is shown in yellow, with the status of each section – footpath or bridleway for example – shown in green underneath (see key on inside front cover). These rights of way markings also indicate the precise alignment of the Coast Path, which walkers should follow. In some cases the yellow line on these maps may show a route which is different from that shown on older maps. Walkers are then recommended to follow the yellow route in this guide, which is that waymarked with the distinctive acorn symbol 🌰 used for all national trails. Any parts of the Coast Path that may be difficult to follow on the ground are clearly highlighted in the route description, and important points to watch for are marked with letters in each chapter, both in the text and on the maps. *Black arrows (➔) at the edge of the maps indicate the start point.* Should there have been a need to alter the route since the publication of this guide, walkers are advised to follow the signs which have been erected on site to indicate this.

KEY MAP 2

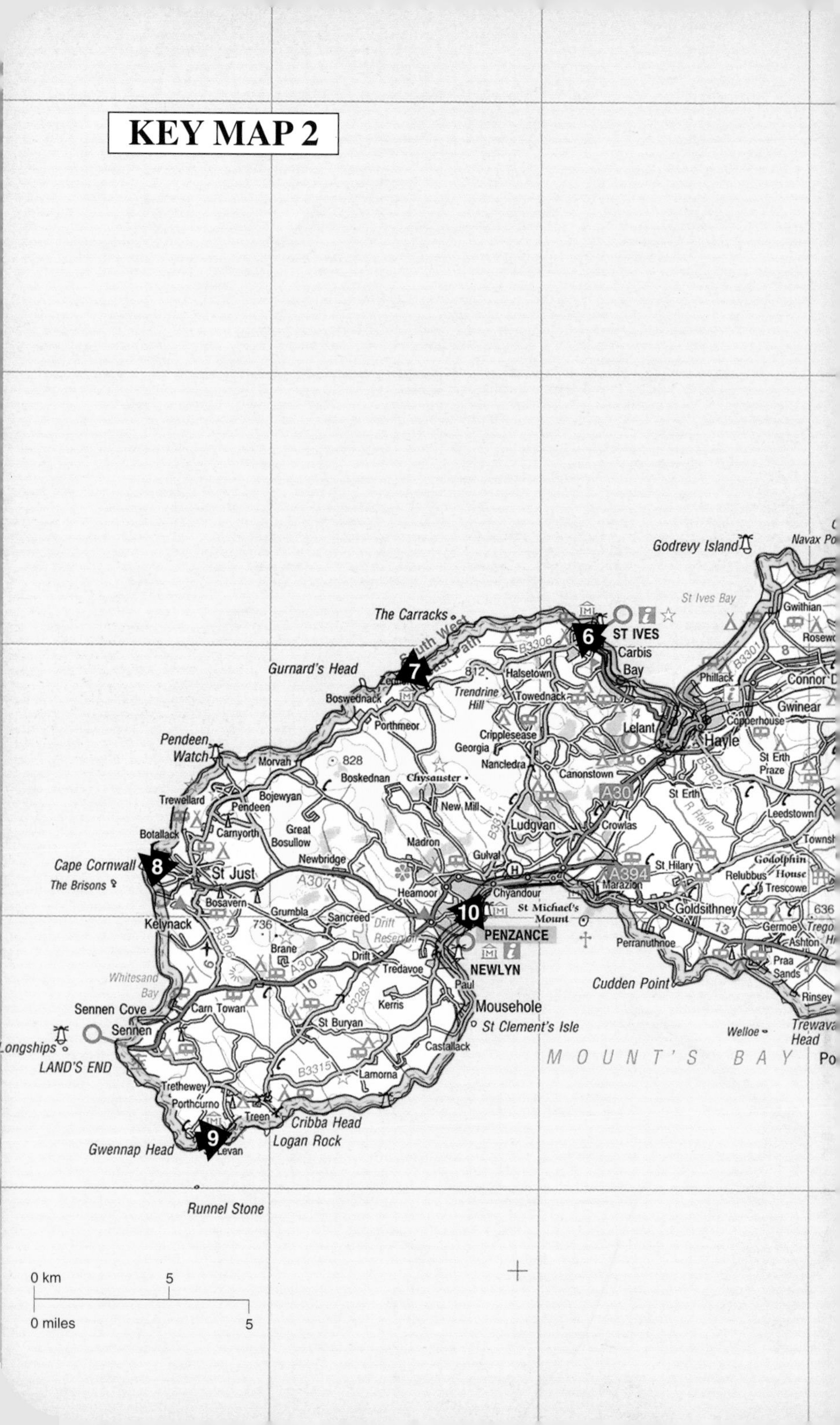

Godrevy Island
Navax Po
St Ives Bay
Gwithian
Rosewo
The Carracks
6 ST IVES
Carbis
Bay
Connor D
Gurnard's Head
7 B12 Halsetown
Phillack
Gwinear
Boswednack Trendrine Hill Towednack
Copperhouse
Porthmeor
Lelant Hayle
St Erth
Praze
Pendeen Watch
Crippleseaze
Georgia
Nancledra
Canonstown
Leedstown
Townsh
Morvah
828
Boskednan
Chysauster
A30
St Erth
Trewellard
Bojewyan
New Mill
Crowlas
St Hilary
Godolphin
House
Relubbus
Trescowe
636
Pendeen
Great
Bosullow
Ludgvan
Botallack
Carnyorth
Madron
Gulval
Marazion
Goldsithney
Cape Cornwall
8 St Just
Newbridge
A3071
Heamoor
Chyandour
St Michael's
Mount
Germoe Trego
Ashton Hi
The Brisons
Bosavern
Perranuthnoe
Kelynack
Grumbla
Sancreed
10
PENZANCE
Praa
Sands
Rinsey
736
Brane
A30
Drift
Reservr
NEWLYN
Cudden Point
Welloe
Trewava
Head
Whitesand
Bay
Tredavoe
Paul
Po
Sennen Cove
Carn Towan
Kerris
Mousehole
St Clement's Isle
M O U N T ' S   B A Y
Longships
Sennen
St Buryan
Castallack
LAND'S END
B3315
Lamorna
Trethewey
Porthcurno
Treen
Cribba Head
Gwennap Head
9 Levan
Logan Rock

Runnel Stone

Distance checklist

This list will assist you in calculating the distances between places on the Coast Path where you may be planning to stay overnight, or in checking your progress along the way.

location	approx. distance from previous location	
	miles	km
Padstow	0	0
Treyarnon Bay Youth Hostel	10.7	17.2
Mawgan Porth	6.8	10.9
Newquay (station)	5.9	9.5
Crantock (by the shortest route)	3.4	5.5
Crantock (via Trevemper Bridge)	8.3	13.4
Perranporth	8.2	13.2
Trevaunance Cove (for St Agnes)	3.7	6.0
Portreath	8.2	13.2
Gwithian	7.7	12.4
Hayle	4.2	6.8
St Ives	5.4	8.7
Zennor Head (for Zennor)	6.6	10.6
Pendeen Watch (for Pendeen)	6.7	10.8
Cape Cornwall (for St Just)	3.9	6.3
Land's End Youth Hostel	1.2	1.9
Sennen Cove	4.0	6.4
Land's End	1.1	1.8
Porthcurno	5.1	8.2
Lamorna Cove	5.2	8.4
Mousehole	2.3	3.7
Penzance	3.6	5.8
Marazion	3.0	4.8
Praa Sands	6.1	9.8
Porthleven	4.1	6.6
Polurrian Cove (for Mullion)	6.2	10.0
Lizard Point (for Lizard town)	7.2	11.6
Cadgwith	3.8	6.1
Coverack	7.1	11.4
Porthoustock	3.5	5.6
Gillan	3.7	6.0
St Antony-in-Meneage (by road)	2.4	3.9
Helford	3.0	4.8
Helford Passage (by road and paths)	8.4	13.5
Falmouth (Albert Quay)	9.6	15.4

Preface

The South West Coast Path follows the spectacular fringe of one of one of Britain's most popular coastal holiday areas, from Minehead in Somerset through Devon and Cornwall, to Poole in Dorset. The section covered in this book, from Padstow to Falmouth, skirts most of the Cornish coast including Carbis Bay and St Ives, Pendeen Watch and Cape Cornwall, Lands End, Penzance, the Lizard Point and the Helford River.

The variety of coastal scenery on this stretch of the path is remarkable, from the long sandy estuary at Hale, to the rocky cliffs of the west coast of Cornwall around Lands End and the pretty harbours of the Lizard peninsula. It is a coastline which is largely defined as Heritage Coast and is predominantly wild and rugged. Circular walks inland make the path attractive to day visitors as well as to the seasoned long-distance walker.

National Trails are promoted and funded by the Countryside Agency and maintained by local authorities. The exposed nature of the South West Coast Path makes this a major undertaking in some areas. Like other National Trails, the path is waymarked with the distinctive acorn symbol which signals that you are on the right route.

I hope that you will enjoy this book during many hours of walking on this delightful stretch of England's coastline.

Ewen Cameron
Chairman
The Countryside Agency

The Armed Knight and Enys Dodnan off Land's End.

PART ONE

Introduction

The landscape along the Coast Path

Many people would say that the stretch of national trail from Padstow, at the mouth of the Camel Estuary, to Falmouth, at the mouth of the River Fal, is the best of the entire South West Coast Path. Along the route you will discover many outstanding views; far too plentiful to indicate on the maps. Its landscape includes sheltered estuaries, countless sea stacks, caves and blasted cliff tops, and its plant and animal life is no less varied. Birds migrate through the area in their thousands each year and the flora and fauna of the Lizard are unique. Apart from such natural splendours, this part of Cornwall has a very long and varied history, geologically, industrially and socially.

A century ago much of the landscape looked very different. There was great industrial activity, with the mining, processing and smelting of ores and the consequent growth of massive waste tips, which resulted in the silting up of rivers and choking of the ports. Then there were the ancillary industries – the foundries casting the great single-cylinder Cornish engines, blacksmiths making miners' tools, and coopers making barrels to contain the ores and the arsenic for export. The list of trades

The 19th century engine house for the Towanwroath shaft of Wheal Coates is one of the many legacies of mining near St Agnes.

was long, and in many places the air would have been sulphurous and smoky, and the noise of the stamps crushing the ore deafening. Today the air is clean, many of the dumps flattened and under cultivation, others naturally recolonised by plants, and the machinery gone. A few engine-houses remain, typically Cornish reminders of industries past.

There is little mining now, but fishing is still of major economic importance, although not due to the traditional pilchard, whose inshore shoals vanished long ago, but to a wide variety of other species. The highest-value catch in England is landed at Newlyn, and fishing provides a source of income for many towns and villages along this section of the national trail.

Cornish history is much more than the story of mining and fishing, of course. Although many of the early historical remains have gone, more survive here than anywhere else in Britain: stone circles, cliff castles, Iron Age villages and ancient field patterns. Although the older historical remains are particularly evident in the far west, so much evidence of Cornwall's history can be seen as you walk from Padstow to Falmouth.

These days tourism is economically important and is under-going a transformation from the traditional view of Cornwall as 'sun, sand and palm trees' to a more discerning view which seeks to protect and conserve the intrinsic values of the county. The tourist industry is broadening its range of attractions, so that visitors can be informed and entertained, when it is too wet or windy for the beach, by everything from heritage coast programmes to well-maintained adventure areas for children. It is important to remember that visitors mean jobs in this eco-nomically deprived region, even if many are only seasonal. Much of the coast is being protected against development by the National Trust's Enterprise Neptune, which was set up to acquire as much as possible of the most beautiful stretches of coastline in England and Wales, and in a few places develop-ment has even been reversed.

Even in the height of summer, though, you will see remark-ably few signs of tourism as you walk the Coast Path. Away from the popular places you will meet few of the millions of visitors that Cornwall absorbs each season – simply the best of the landscapes and seascapes, and a proud and fascinating history written into the countryside.

Practical advice

The days when the intrepid walkers of the Coast Path carried sharp implements in order to cut a path – was it the right one? – through gorse, bracken, blackthorn and brambles have thank-fully gone. The Countryside Agency awards grants to the high-way authority to maintain the path and improve the waymark-ing. It is still possible to get lost, but if you follow the maps and the instructions in this guide you should have little trouble finding your way.

If the waymarks indicate a different route from the one shown on the map, then do follow the waymarks. The sea may have eroded the coast, necessitating a diversion, or the route may have been improved. Better routes are being negotiated so that some of the inland stretches can be replaced by a truly coastal path.

The real problem for the walker can be finding accommoda-tion or returning to the starting point of a walk. Accommodation becomes heavily booked during the summer, but even then a few telephone calls will find you bed and breakfast accommoda-tion. In winter much of the tourist industry shuts down: hotels, bed and breakfast accommodation, youth hostels, National

Trust sites, cafés on the coast, even public conveniences are locked up. Most of the cafés along the trail that open all year round are mentioned in the text, but they may not be open in a wet south-westerly gale, when you need them most.

The perennial problem for those who are walking for just one day is how to return to their vehicles, or directly to their homes. Public transport is best in summer, but even then it is somewhat skeletal, which is why the sections of the trail often begin and end in the more important towns and villages. The county council's compendium of public transport services gives the best help – details are given in the Useful Information section of this guide.

The only section of the trail where real planning is essential is the length from St Ives to Sennen Cove. This is very exposed, and food, water, toilets and accommodation are all located inland.

No matter which part of the coast you are walking and no matter for how long, you should wear well broken-in boots or shoes that give a good grip. Carry waterproofs and a spare warm garment, adequate liquids and food, a small first-aid kit, and a whistle (six blasts is the emergency signal), but dispense with all non-essentials because all this gear has to be carried on your shoulders. Do take binoculars if you can, so that you can watch the seals and the peregrines, see the ruins on land and the wrecks in the coves, and, where there are many tracks, look for the acorn waymarks on short posts that indicate the way ahead.

The weather on the two coasts of Cornwall can be quite different. You can obtain an inshore weather forecast from Marinecall (01891 500458) and a regional forecast from Weathercheck (09001 112248).

Safety precautions

High winds can make walking slow and tiring, and very high winds can make it dangerous along much of the cliff, if close to the edges. Also strong onshore winds carry spray far inland. Swimming can be hazardous from many superb-looking beaches, especially at low water. Many beaches have powerful rip currents that carry water away from the beach: if you have the misfortune to be caught in one of these, swim diagonally to the current into stiller water, before turning to head back to the beach. The more popular beaches have lifeguards on duty in the season, and the area for safe bathing lies between the yellow and red flags.

Remember too that every year people are washed off rocks and drowned, and every year people are cut off by the tide and have to be rescued. The lifeguards will let you know the time of high water, and it is also given in the local weather forecast on television, as well as in local newspapers.

The coastguards are responsible for dealing with any emergency that occurs on the coast or at sea. To contact them dial 999 and ask for the coastguard. Please remember that there are no coastguard lookouts now, and the service relies on the watchful eyes of the public. If you see vessels or people you think are in distress, dial 999.

Newquay Harbour at low tide.

PART TWO

SOUTH WEST COAST PATH
Padstow to Falmouth

1 Padstow to Treyarnon Bay

via Trevone and Trevose Head
10¾ miles (17.2 km)

If you have crossed the Camel Estuary, the ferry will normally have dropped you at North Quay **1** in Padstow, but if the tide was low you will be left at Lower Beach **2**. There is information on all the ferries used along the route on page 133–6.

The Coast Path leaves the harbour by the slope **A** beside the discreet red brick toilets on North Quay Parade. The tarmac path continues to a modern granite cross, the war memorial, passing a notice pointing out that the ferry crosses at low tide from Lower Beach, which is down a track and then steps. Beyond the war memorial the path is a veritable highway to the very sheltered St George's Cove **3**.

Gun Point **4** has a bolted cast-iron tank dated 1888 and a war-department granite marker dated 1868, but was already called Gun Point on the Ordnance Survey Map of 1801. The site is listed, among others, as being fortified against the Armada, although it is not known if this was ever carried out.

The Coast Path is carried on boards through the marsh at the head of Harbour Cove **5**. This area, where marsh orchids now grow, had moorings for boats in the 1920s before the main channel of the Camel straightened, going north from Gun Point to Trebetherick Point on the eastern side. If the tide is out you can cross the dunes and the good sandy beach at Harbour Cove, known locally as Tregirls.

The changing sand-banks in the estuary led to the removal of the lifeboat from its base at Hawker's Cove. The path skirts the converted lifeboat house and joins the road for a few yards at the back of the beach. The older terrace, with chimneys set at an angle, was built in 1874 for the pilots, while the newer houses, made of white brick from North Devon, were used by the coast-guards. In order to help vessels make the safety of Padstow without being driven on to the Doom Bar, capstans were installed in the lee of Stepper Point and ships warped round. The outline of Stepper has been much altered by quarrying.

As you leave the sheltered side of the estuary and start the walk down the coast, the change in scenery is dramatic. A little way on, and in spring among a carpet of squill, is a stone tower **6**, built in 1832 by the Association for the Preservation of Life and Property as a daymark to help guide ships into the Camel.

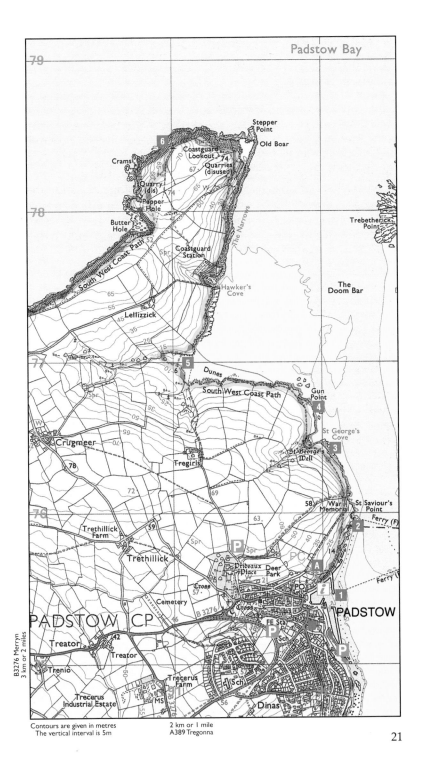

Padstow Bay

Stepper
Point

Old Boar

6 Coastguard
Lookout
74
Quarries
(disused)
Crams
67

Quarry
(dis)
Pepper
al Hole

Butter's
Hole

Coastguard
Station

Trebetherick
Point

South West Coast Path

Hawker's
Cove

The
Doom Bar

Lellizzick

Dunes

5

South West Coast Path

Gun
Point

4

Crugmeer

St George's
Cove

3

Tregirls

St George's
Well

War
Memorial

St Saviour's
Point

Ferry (F)

Trethillick
Farm

2

Prideaux
Place

Deer
Park

P

PC

A

Ferry (F)

i **1**

PO

PADSTOW

PADSTOW CP

Cemetery

Cross

Cross

B 3276

FE Sta

P
Sch

P

Treator

Treator

Trenio

Trecerus
Farm

Sch

Trecerus
Industrial Estate

MS

Dinas

B3276 Merryn
3 km or 2 miles

Contours are given in metres
The vertical interval is 5m

2 km or 1 mile
A389 Tregonna

Just east of Fox Hole **7** the permissive circular walk back to Padstow leaves the coast, and just beyond is the beginning of a large guillemot and razorbill colony stretching to Porthmissen.

Most of the rock along the coast in North Cornwall is slate, apart from occasional igneous rock headlands, but at Marble Cliffs **8**, Porthmissen, there is limestone – a rarity here. There are more than 80 beds of limestone with shale between the layers, just as in the much younger Jurassic Lias, found in a belt from Lyme Regis in Dorset to Whitby in Yorkshire, but here there are no ammonites or icthyosaurs, and the whole sequence is upside-down, as well as being very localised. Another nearby geological curiosity is the Round Hole, a collapsed sea-cave: you can find out more from the geology guide available in the shop. Further on, people in wheelchairs can now enjoy the view from St Cadoc's Point **9**. Under Harlyn Inn there is the site of an Iron Age cemetery that held more than a hundred crouched skeletons; the finds from the area are now in the museum in Truro.

Erosion along several geological faults has produced the Merope Islands.

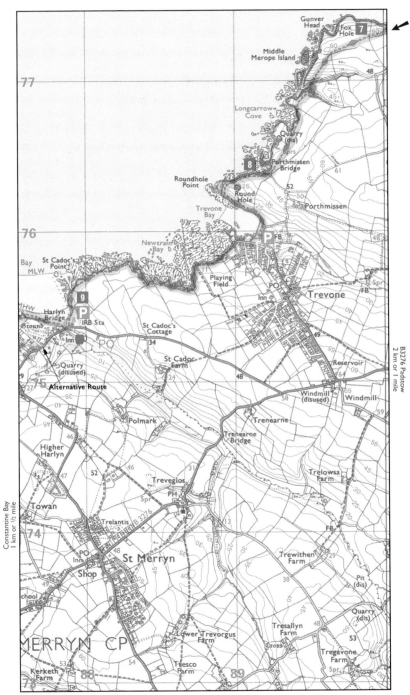

Contours are given in metres
The vertical interval is 5m

The path westwards from Harlyn Bridge currently follows the beach for a short distance, but at the highest spring tides it may be necessary to go inland along the road through the hamlet of Harlyn to the village of Constantine Bay then take the path to the beach at Constantine Bay **12**. The Cellars are old fish cellars and date from the days when Harlyn Bay was the site of a pilchard seine. The inscription over the door – LUCRI DULCIS ODOR – can be translated as 'Sweet is the smell of riches'! More information on pilchards can be found on page 51.

The old quarries **10** at Cataclews Point are now the site of a sewage treatment works. The distinctive Cataclews stone was used by the Master of St Endellion in the 14th century to carve the fonts in Padstow and St Merryn churches. The stone is a variety of dolerite, a rock often called 'blue elvan' by Cornish quarrymen, to distinguish it from the usual 'elvan', which is a fine-grained granite often associated with metal lodes.

Another dolerite forms Merope Rocks, where ravens nest and which shelters Padstow's new lifeboat station. Before the move in 1967 Padstow had lost three lifeboats on the Doom Bar. This station is not open to visitors, unlike all the other stations between here and Falmouth.

Trevose Head Lighthouse **11** was opened in 1847 to fill in the gap between the Longships and the old Lundy light.

The path now turns south, crossing the back of the beach at Constantine Bay **12**, where work is continuing to protect the sand dunes. Swimming can be hazardous both here and at Treyarnon Bay **13**, where there is a youth hostel, a caravan site, and a hotel.

Padstow

'This is one of those antiquated unsavoury fishing-towns which are viewed most agreeably from a distance', according to Murray's 1859 *Guide to Devon and Cornwall*. The reeking pilchard palaces are long disused, but Padstow is still a fishing town, with most of its activity open to view on the southern side of the harbour. In summer the town is visited by tourists and is still a pleasantly antiquated place to explore.

St Petroc, a much revered Welsh missionary, founded a monastery here in the 7th century, which was moved to Bodmin in 981 after a Viking raid.

The Camel Estuary forms a rare natural harbour on the dangerous north Cornish coast, and Padstow grew as a centre for shipbuilding, trade and fishing. The safety of the harbour became illusory, however, because of the growth of the great sandbar, the Doom Bar, at its mouth, on which 300 vessels are known to have been wrecked or stranded in the 150 years to the beginning of this century, and countless more before. The sand is composed of broken shells, so hundreds of thousands of tons were taken away to improve the sour acidic soils of Cornwall, although today crushed limestone from upcountry has largely replaced the shell sand.

Nowadays Padstow is best known for its 'Obby 'Osses on May Day. Even St Petroc, St Wethinoc, St Samson and St Cadoc might not be able to dampen the pagan gusto of this celebration of the return of summer.

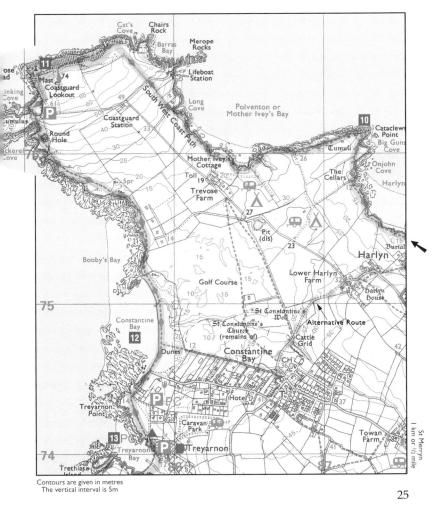

Contours are given in metres
The vertical interval is 5m

Circular walks from Padstow

6½ miles (10.5 km)

There are several circular routes from Padstow along the Coast Path past Stepper Point. These take about half a day to complete. The permissive route below leaves the Coast Path near Fox Hole **7**, there are also good routes back from Trevone.

Park in Padstow at the southern end of the outer harbour then walk past the Shipwreck Museum to North Quay **1** and the start of the Coast Path **A**. Follow the Coast Path to near Fox Hole **7** (see pages 20 and 22). Cross the stile and walk along the permissive path at the edge of the field to the road that joins Padstow and Hawker's Cove. Now walk to Crugmeer, where there was once an aerodrome, turn left at the junction in Crugmeer, pass a few houses, then take the footpath to Padstow across the fields. Some of these fields are farmed for cereals, so please observe the country code when crossing them. After the seventh field you join the lane from Tregirls to Padstow and walk down this under an archway and past Prideaux Place, a small Elizabethan manor house with a deer park and beautifully restored long gallery, open to visitors in the summer. Then continue down Fentonluna Lane to the harbour.

Two shorter variations of this walk are also well-trodden: you either leave the Coast Path on the south side of Harbour Cove **5** and return through the farm of Tregirls, or you follow the road from Hawker's Cove through Lellizzick and Crugmeer. Harbour Cove, usually known as Tregirls, is a good safe beach with

The Coast Path leaves Padstow Harbour near the Red Brick building.

26

acres of sand at low water, backed by sand dunes, so the shortest route plus time at the beach would make a good day for a family with young children.

A third alternative would be a walk along the flat Camel Trail, which follows the line of the old railway beside the River Camel from the old railway station in the car park to Bodmin, and on further to Wenfordbridge.

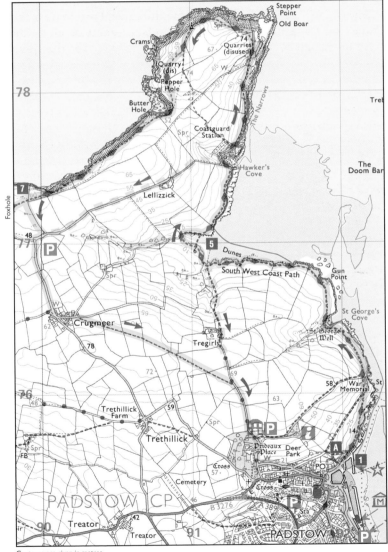

Contours are given in metres
The vertical interval is 5m

2 Treyarnon Bay to Newquay

via Mawgan Porth and Griffin's Point
12¾ miles (20.4 km)

Treyarnon Bay **13** is very dangerous for swimming at low water because of a strong current, which will take you out to sea, so instead use the 'swimming pool' in the rocks on the north-east side.

Immediately south of Trethias Island are what appear to be three Iron Age cliff castles **14**, which in fact are one, but erosion has cut the coves, and separated the defensive bank into three sections. Erosion is still proceeding rapidly, so take care. The remains of the *Hemsley I* are visible at low tide in Fox Cove. She was an aged tanker on her last voyage to the breaker's yard at Antwerp when she struck in a gale in 1969 and sank.

Soon the path turns inland to Porthcothan, which has suffered rather lopsided development; the northern side is owned by the National Trust (NT) and has not been built on. The route follows the road for a few yards, then turns back to the beach past a useful shop and post office. There is also a pub, phone box, public conveniences and a bus stop.

The path skirts the seaward side of the houses towards Trescore Islands. In one small cove **15** there are some man-made caves, and various spikes embedded in the rock: relics of smuggling, or of unloading and dismembering a wreck? Park Head **16**, owned by the NT, has a spectacularly sited cliff castle, as well as a large area in imminent danger of slipping down the cliff and into the sea.

Park Head attracts a few visitors, those who like fresh air and spectacular views, but Bedruthan Steps **17** is a tourist honeypot. The Steps are owned by the Carnanton Estate and were developed as a tourist attraction by the Victorians after the railway reached Newquay in 1875. The NT has a property called Carnewas to the south and has tackled the erosion problem there by building a path leading to a viewing platform looking out over the Steps. The NT car park is surrounded by a Cornish hedge, and the NT also has a small NT shop and a deservedly popular tea-shop open from spring to autumn. The slate stacks include Queen Bess, who lost her head a few years ago, as you will realise if you see old photographs, and Samaritan Island, the site of the wreck of a ship called the *Samaritan*, which indeed gave succour to the local population.

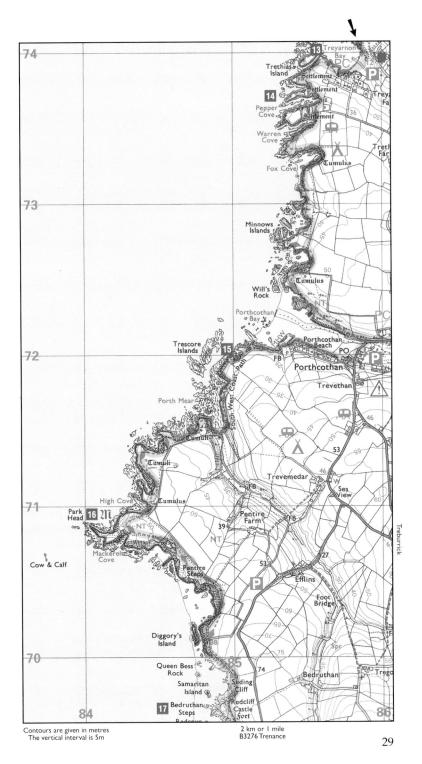

74

13 Treyarnon
Bay
PC
P

Trethias
Island
Settlement
Trey
Fa

14
Settlement

Pepper
Cove
Settlement
36

Warren
Cove
Treth
Far

Fox Cove
Tumulus

73

Minnows
Islands
45

Tumulus

Will's
Rock
50
NT
PC

Porthcothan
Bay
Porthcothan
Beach
PO

72
Trescore
Islands
15
Porthcothan
FB

Porth Mear
Trevethan
30

35

40
46

Tumuli

Tumuli
53

Trevemedar
46

High Cove
Tumulus
FB
Sea
View
60

71
Park
Head
16 ᛘ
NT
Pentire
Farm
FB
39
NT

27
Cow & Calf
Mackerels
Cove
Pentire
Steps
53

Efflins

P
Foot
Bridge

Diggory's
Island

70
Queen Bess
Rock
85
74
Bedruthan
Trego
Samaritan
Island
Sliding
Cliff
Redcliff
Castle
Fort
17 Bedruthan
Steps

84
86

Contours are given in metres
The vertical interval is 5m

2 km or 1 mile
B3276 Trenance

Treburrick

29

The path descends from Trenance Point to Mawgan Porth past a strange linear depression **18** in which two garden sheds nestle. This depression is part of a canal intended to link Mawgan Porth, St Columb and Porth (now part of Newquay) and to carry mainly sea-sand to 'afford the means of improving many thousand acres of barren and unprofitable ground'. It was also intended to carry coal inland and St Columb stone for export. The canal was never finished, although the section from Trenance to St Columb was completed by 1779.

Mawgan Porth has a car park, toilets, shops, hotels and a bus service. Up the valley is the village of St Mawgan with some of the best memorial brasses in Cornwall in the church. Nearby is St Mawgan Airfield, with both a military helicopter repair base and Cornwall's major civil airport sharing the same site. The Coast Path joins the beach at the northern end of the dunes **A**. These dunes are undergoing restoration and people are restricted to fenced paths through them. The path is becoming hazardous in places because of erosion.

Griffin's Point **19** has a well-preserved cliff castle into which the path just cuts. Many of the headlands in the south-west have cliff castles, which are also known as promontory forts and which date from the Iron Age, approximately the 4th century BC to the Romano–British time. To the south of the castle is Stem Cove, thought to be the site of the last nesting place of choughs in Cornwall. Choughs are considered by the Cornish to be their national emblem, and indeed one stands on top of the coat of arms of the county of Cornwall. Choughs have suffered a long decline, having been abundant all along the south coast from Dover to Cornwall in the 17th century; but by 1802 they were chiefly confined to Devon, Cornwall and Wales. The last resident Cornish chough died in 1973 and their numbers are decreasing in Wales too. Many people would support an attempt to reintroduce them, but the reasons for their decline need to be understood first. A major reason seems to have been loss of habitat (choughs are probers and need short, well-grazed turf in which to find their food), but human interference also played a part.

The path now starts the long sweep of Watergate Bay, which ends in Newquay. The bay is sandy and good for surfing, and the rocks are the oldest on the path between Padstow and Falmouth (apart from the Lizard). They contain fragments of early jawless fish almost 400 million years old, which appear to have sucked up their food from the bottom of rivers and lakes.

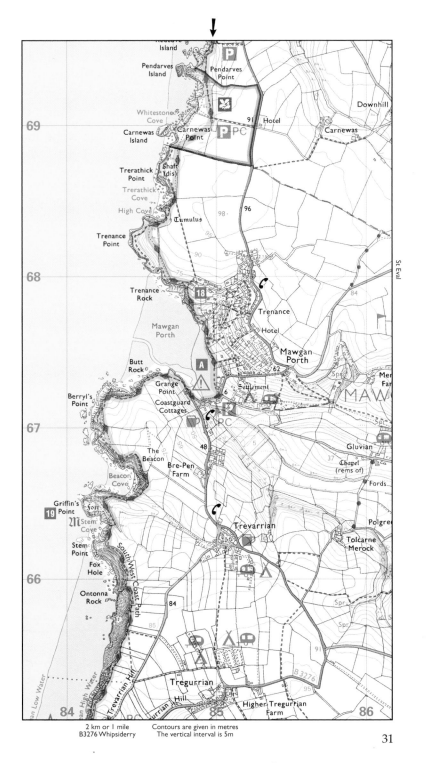

Redeye
Island

P

Pendarves
Island

Pendarves
Point

Whitestone
Cove

91 Hotel

Downhill

Carnewas
Island

Carnewas
Point

P PC

Carnewas

69

Trerathick
Point

Shaft
(dis)

Trerathick
Cove

High Cove

Tumulus

98   96

Trenance
Point

90

75

St Eval

Trenance
Rock

18

68

Mawgan
Porth

Trenance

84

Hotel

Mawgan
Porth

Butt
Rock

A

62

Spr

Mer
Far

Berryl's
Point

Grange
Point

Settlement

MAW

Coastguard
Cottages

PC

6

67

The
Beacon

48

37

Gluvian

Beacon
Cove

Bre-Pen
Farm

Chapel
(rems of)

Fords

Griffin's
Point

19

Fort

Stem
Cove

Trevarrian

Polgre

Stem
Point

Tolcarne
Merock

Fox
Hole

66

Ontonna
Rock

84

85

91

Spr

South West Coast Path

Spr

Tregurrian
Hill

B 3276

95

Trevarrian Hill

Higher Tregurrian
Farm

Mean Low Water

Mean High Water

84

85

86

The path snakes around two large tumuli and then descends to Porth passing Trevelgue Head, the most heavily defended cliff castle in Cornwall, leading archaeologists to suspect that before Porth silted up it was an important landing place. As well as the seven ramparts, evidence of bronze and iron smelting has been found and the site was occupied, discontinuously, from at least the 3rd century BC to the 6th century AD. The next ancient site is Barrowfields **20**, so called because of the three Bronze Age barrows. After this you follow the road until you reach the pedestrian way, The Tram Track, **B** leading seawards shortly after the railway station. This takes you to the main bus station, and then you follow Bank Street and Fore Street to North Quay Hill and the harbour **21**. Nowadays Newquay is an unashamed holiday town, but its history includes the pilchard fishery, silver-lead mining, and it was the industrial port for the Treffry family, one of the major families involved in the development of the china clay industry.

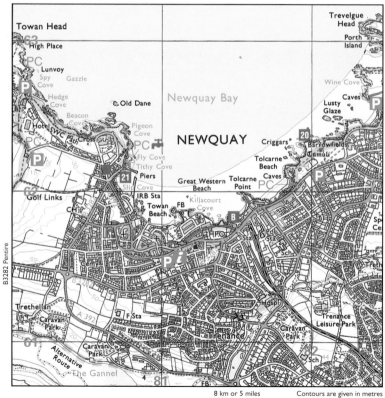

8 km or 5 miles
A3075 Goonhavern

Contours are given in metres
The vertical interval is 5m

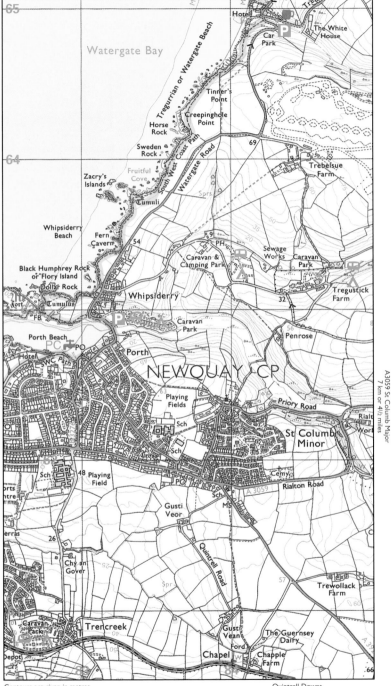

Contours are given in metres
The vertical interval is 5m

Quintrell Downs

3 Newquay to Perranporth

across the Gannel and past Penhale Camp
11½ miles (18.5 km)

The route to Perranporth is relatively easy, but includes crossing the Gannel, and 1 miles (2 km) along Perran Beach.

From Newquay harbour **21** the Coast Path is waymarked up the steps from the north side of the quay, past the whitewashed Huer's Hut **22** (see page 51) and round a prominent hotel on Towan Head to Fistral Beach, well known to surfers.

To cross the Gannel there are four possible bridges, and one ferry (see page 133) but your choice will be restricted by the time of day, the month, the state of the tide, the weather and sea conditions. At the south end of Fistral Beach **A** the recommended route takes you left, east, along Pentire Road then down Pentire Crescent, along the recently developed Penmere Drive and Trevean Way and across the green to the Gannel at the bottom of Trethellan Hill **B**. Here you can cross the tidal bridge to the mouth of Penpol Creek **C**.

If you cannot cross here, walk upstream along the path between the houses and the river to the next tidal bridge **D** just before Trenance boating lake. This bridge is higher, and remem-

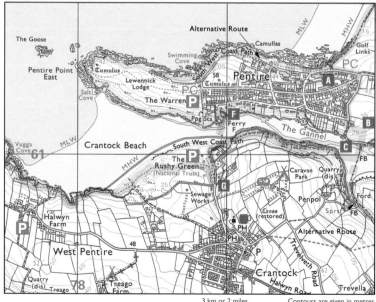

3 km or 2 miles
Cubert

Contours are given in metres
The vertical interval is 5m

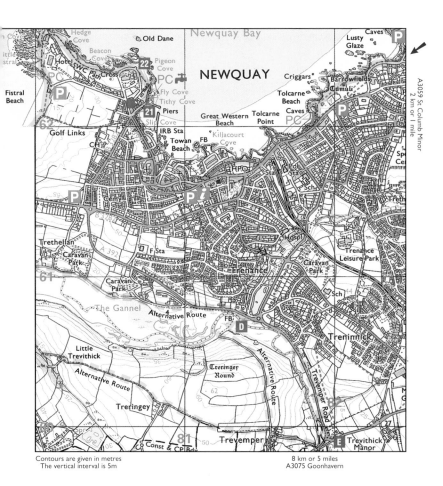

Contours are given in metres
The vertical interval is 5m

8 km or 5 miles
A3075 Goonhavern

ber you have to cross the low-lying salt-marsh beyond to reach the route up to Trevemper (a permissive path along the edge of the estuary back to the mouth of Penpol Creek **C** may be available). If bridge **D** is not usable you will need to continue along Gannel Road and the A3075 to Trevemper Bridge **E** then back through Trevemper, Treringey and Little Trevithick to Penpol Creek **C**.

The final option is to use the private tidal bridge or the ferry at Fern Pit **F**. To reach this you turn right, west, at the south end of Fistral Beach **A** down Esplanade Road and Riverside Crescent to Fern Pit Café, where, if the café is open, you can walk down through the café's garden and cross the river either by the tidal bridge or by ferry. However you cross the Gannel you should make your way to Rushey Green car park **G**.

(From the Rushey Green car park **G**, if you wish to use the Fern Pit ferry or bridge **F**, walk to the bottom of the car park and go between the sand dunes and the cliffs. If you wish to use another crossing, leave the car park about one-third of the way down and walk along the path to Penpol **C**. If you cannot cross from there, or by Trenance **D**, you will need to walk up the track to Trevemper Bridge **E**.)

Rushey Green is a mass of tracks, so head westwards until you reach the National Trust boundary and a signpost for the Coast Path. This heads round Pentire Point West into Porth Joke, a sheltered cove and lagoon, where you may see herons. Locally it is known as Polly Joke. Depending on the tides you can miss Holywell by fording the stream at the landward end of the cliffs and taking the stile **H** into Penhale Camp.

From Holywell, known for its holy wells and also its ancient pub, the Treguth, the path skirts the seaward edge of Penhale Camp and then follows Perran Beach to Perranporth.

Prominent red signs emphasise the lack of facilities between Holywell and Perranporth and also the need to keep to the path, avoid short cuts, and obey sentries posted on the rifle range. The path around the camp is marked by white-painted posts which, as far as possible, should be on your landward side. The cliff castle **23** on Penhale Point consists of two impressive ramparts across a steep slope. The rusty-looking Perran Iron Lode shows up clearly at the back of the old quarry **24** below the

Holywell Bay.

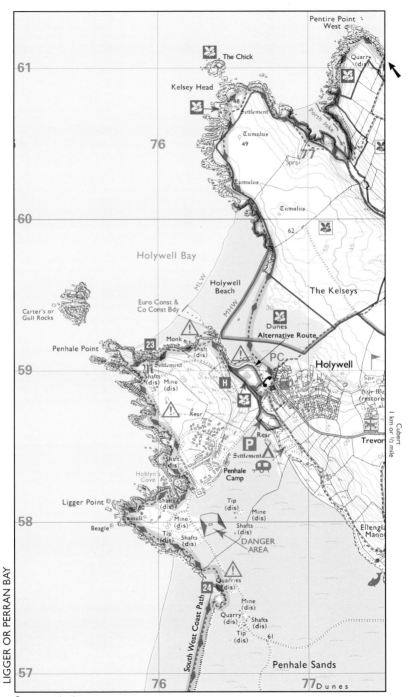

LIGGER OR PERRAN BAY

Pentire Point West

Quarry (dis)

The Chick

Kelsey Head

48 Settlement

Porth Joke

Tumulus 49

Tumulus

Spr

77

Tumulus

Tumulus

62

55 45

Holywell Bay

MLW

Holywell Beach

The Kelseys

Carter's or Gull Rocks

Euro Const & Co Const Bdy

MHW

30

Dunes
Alternative Route

Penhale Point

Monk

23

Shaft (dis)

PC

Holywell

Settlement

Shafts (dis)

Shafts (dis)

Mine (dis)

H

Holy W (restore)

Resr

Spr

Trevor

Resr

Shaft (dis)

Settlement

P

Penhale Camp

Hoblyn's Cove

Shafts (dis)

Ligger Point

60

Shafts (dis)

Tip (dis)

Mine (dis)

Tumuli

Mine (dis)

Ellengl
Mano

Beagle

Tip (dis)

Shafts (dis)

DANGER AREA

South West Coast Path

24

Quarries (dis)

Mine (dis)

Quarry (dis)

Shafts (dis)

Tip (dis)

61

Penhale Sands

76

77 Dunes

Cubert
1 km or ½ mile

Contours are given in metres
The vertical interval is 5m

37

path at the north end of Perran Beach. The path follows the back of the beach: the dunes and the whole of Penhale Sands are Ministry of Defence property and out of bounds. The ruined 12th century St Piran's Church **25**, site of the Domesday monastery of Lanpiran, can be visited, but St Piran's Oratory, probably the oldest church in Cornwall, was in a poor, usually flooded state, even within its protecting concrete bunker, and has been reburied beneath the sand. The black and white flag often seen flying in Cornwall bears the cross of St Piran, who shares with St Petroc and St Michael the role of Cornwall's patron saint.

At low water you can walk to Perranporth along the beach, possibly admiring the sand yachts, but at high water the sea reaches the foot of the cliffs at Cotty's Point, and you need to walk through the sand dunes, bearing right between the cliffs and the holiday centre and golf links. If you are heading south, the last safe exit from the beach is by concrete steps **I** just south of the adit, with more concrete steps **J** taking the footpath down to the beach south of Cotty's Point and into Perranporth. (If you are heading north, you will find the steps **J** down to the beach located at the seaward end of the fenced path that comes from the holiday camp.) The path continues through the dunes, turning seaward down a 'valley' between sand dunes. In Perranporth there is a large car park at the back of the beach. The youth hostel is the single-storey ex-Admiralty building on Droskyn Point, while the more imposingly military building nearby is a block of flats, recently known as Droskyn Castle Hotel.

Crantock

Crantock was the site of the monastery of Langorroc mentioned in *Domesday*. The rather odd appearance of the church, which was ornately restored at the turn of the century, bears witness to its dual use by monks and lay people. The stocks now in the churchyard were last used about 1817, when they were in the church tower, but you may prefer to stop a while in the Old Albion pub close by.

Residents of Crantock are very aware that their village has had a far longer and more glorious history than Newquay, which did not start to grow until the railway brought the tourists. Trading vessels came into Porth, to the north of Newquay, or up the Gannel to the south. Possibly connected to shipping are several man-made depressions in the slate a little upstream of the Fern Pit crossing, and clearly visible from the Crantock side.

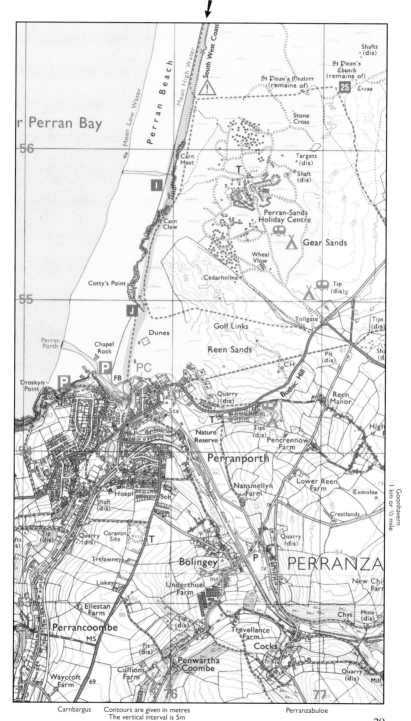

r Perran Bay

Perran Beach

Mean Low Water

Mean High Water

South West Coast

56

55

Carn Haut

Carn Clew

Cotty's Point

Chapel Rock

Perran Porth

Droskyn Point

Dunes

FB

PC

St Piran's Church (remains of)

Cross

St Piran's Oratory (remains of)

Stone Cross

Shafts (dis)

Targets (dis)

Shaft (dis)

Perran-Sands Holiday Centre

Gear Sands

Wheal Vlow

Cedarholme

Tip (dis)

Golf Links

Reen Sands

Tollgate

Tips (dis)

Pit (dis)

Sha (d

CH

Budnic Hill

Reen Manor

Quarry (dis)

Nature Reserve

Tips (dis)

Pencrennow Farm

High

Perranporth

Nansmellyn Farm

Lower Reen Farm

Tumulus

Crestlands

Hospl

Sch

Shaft (dis)

Quarry (dis)

Caravan Site

T

Quarry (dis)

PERRANZA

Trelawney

Bolingey

Liskey

Underthuel Farm

Inn

P

New Chi Farm

Ellestan Farm

Chys

Mine (dis)

Perrancoombe

MS

Tip (dis)

Pit (dis)

Trevellance Farm

Cocks

Quarry (dis)

Mill

Waycroft Farm

Cullions Farm

Penwartha Coombe

76

77

Carnbargus

Contours are given in metres
The vertical interval is 5m

Perranzabuloe

Goonhavern
I km or ½ mile

39

Pressures on the Coast Path

The Coast Path is a narrow strip of land that is the property of some individuals, trusts, estates, the armed forces or a company. In many places the land is used for stock-rearing or growing crops, so the narrower the path made by walkers and their dogs, the better for the farmers. On the seaward side the land is being worn away slowly, or is slipping away in great chunks, taking fences, paths, road signs and even roads, so that negotiations are needed to reinstate the path further inland. Partly as a result of problems with thoughtless walkers and their dogs, which worry stock, the path and all the land seaward of it has been fenced off in places; in other areas it is purely for stock control. The sad result is that blackthorn, brambles, bracken and gorse grow to form scrubland. On the Lizard English Nature and the National Trust are managing the coastal strip by cutting the scrub and using Shetland ponies and Soay sheep to eat the regrowth.

A different problem is most evident at Land's End and Bedruthan Steps, where humans are a major agent of erosion

Nearly all of the Coast Path between Padstow and Falmouth is as pleasant to walk as this stretch north of Zennor.

and large areas of bare soil are exposed, to blow away in a dry summer, leaving a gravelly surface. Erosion is also a major problem in coastal sand dunes, which become stabilised naturally, except where trampling stops the process. Here the British Trust for Conservation Volunteers and other groups are planting marram grass and keeping walkers on a Dutch ladder between fences, so giving the dunes a chance to stabilise rapidly. Further problems come with mountain bikes, trials bikes and all-terrain vehicles, which are not authorised on footpaths but permitted on byways. Mountain bikes and horses can also use bridleways, but very little of the Coast Path is either bridleway or byway.

If you are walking the Coast Path on a beautiful sunny day with a gentle breeze and the sea looking like a millpond, you may feel that the path is over-waymarked, and a long way back from the cliff edge. This seems over-zealous in its caution, but please remember that others will be walking at the same spot on another day when a sea mist has rolled in and visibility drops to a few yards.

4 Perranporth to Portreath

past St Agnes and Porthtowan
12 miles (19.3 km)

This is an easy walk following well-used paths across the flat top of the cliffs, with occasional valleys to cross. You are never very far from the road, a pub, public conveniences and shops.

From Perranporth, the Coast Path follows the hill up Cliff Road, then goes behind the castellated hotel and the youth hostel and on to the cliff top. (If you are heading north and looking for the hostel, you should find a sign where the hostel path branches off to the left.)

The coast from Perranporth to Porthtowan has as much evidence of mining as anywhere in Cornwall, although currently the area around Levant, Geevor and Botallack has more in the way of interpretation for the visitor. Much of the evidence

Contours are given in metres
The vertical interval is 5m

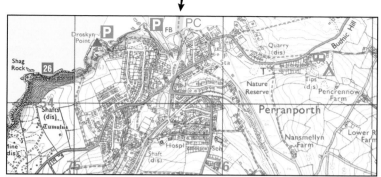

Contours are given in metres
The vertical interval is 5m

Bolingey

here has been destroyed by the elements or by man. For example, if you look east from the track **26** near Shag Rock, the old men's workings can be seen riddling the slate cliffs. The area around Cligga Head draws people with many interests; geologists, mineral-hunters, rock-climbers, and glider pilots, whose club house **27** is part of the buildings of the old British and Colonial Explosives factory. The airfield dates from the Second World War and is little changed, but the relics of the explosives factory and of the processing works for the tin mines are far less easy to disentangle. Cligga Mine yielded tungsten as well as tin and, like many tungsten producers, was worked in the last war to supply tungsten for armour-plating and armour-piercing shells. In the early 1980s the mine was sampled again, but the programme stopped when the price of tin dropped from more than £10,000 per tonne to less than £4,000 in 1985.

Hanover Cove **28** is named after the Falmouth packet boat that was carrying gold coins valued at £60,000 when she was wrecked here in 1763. Her royal coat of arms is now in Falmouth Maritime Museum. Above the cove you may be able to find a large granite boundstone marking the edge of a 'sett', an area of ground granted to a group of men willing to prospect for ore.

Bats, including the rare Greater Horseshoe, live inside the disused mines, and conical mesh caps have been put over old shafts to make them safe, but still allow the bats access. Please do not drop stones into the shafts to see how deep they are.

When you reach Trevellas 'porth' or cove **29**, look up the valley, which still has evidence of mining and tin-smelting from medieval times to the present (see page 50). The path follows the east side of the valley before crossing the bridge by the Blue Hills engine house and then you are on the track **30** used every Easter for the London to Land's End motor trials.

St Agnes Beacon rises above the level of the flat-topped cliffs.

Trevaunance Cove used to have St Agnes Harbour on its west side. Here coal was raised by a horse-powered whim, and ore went down a chute from the ore-bins **31**, which are still visible. An unrepaired gap in the breakwater in 1915 resulted in the harbour becoming a mass of scattered granite blocks on the sea bed. There is a good pub near the coast here and you will find many more facilities, including buses, in St Agnes. The St Agnes Museum Trust occupies what was the chapel of ease **32** in the cemetery, and there are guided walks in summer.

From the pub in Trevaunance Cove you start to climb up the valley-side by the steep lane opposite, but then you take the hard-to-find little track behind the block of flats and will find yourself back on a lane above the cove; the open cliff top is not far away. Above Polberro Cove was Polberro Mine, famous for the richness of its tin ore.

Offshore, Bawden Rocks, or Man and his man, have a bird colony that includes guillemots, razorbills and black-backed gulls. Puffins have been seen, and may still breed here. Around Newdowns Head **33** grey seals breed in the caves: the pups are born in November or early December.

St Agnes now has a Voluntary Marine Conservation Area in recognition of the diversity of its marine life. Seashore safaris are run during summer months.

The cliff top on both sides of the coastguard station **34** is a favoured spot for hang-gliders and flyers of radio-controlled model gliders, because of the up-draughts from the cliffs produced by any wind between north and north-west.

On the rocks around the National Trust-owned St Agnes Beacon there are some geologically very young sands and clays (less than 50 million years old). The sand has been worked for centuries and is mostly used for making moulds. Large quantities went from Doble's Pit **35**, and other quarries, to the foundries, such as those at Hayle (see page 62). Clay from St Agnes was puddled (walked all over when wet) to make a waterproof base when the piers were being built in Penzance harbour. However, clay was mostly used to attach candles to miners' felt hats, or to rock, when working underground – the pits **36** behind Beacon Cottage Farm supplied this. Bernard Leach, who made many of his pots in St Ives, also used clay from St Agnes.

To the west are the much photographed remains of Wheal Coates **37**, with the cliff-top view now accessible to wheelchair users. If you walk back up the beach at low tide from Chapel Porth, with its public conveniences and excellent café (try a 'hedgehog'!), you can see in the cliffs an adit and one of the lodes that was worked by this mine.

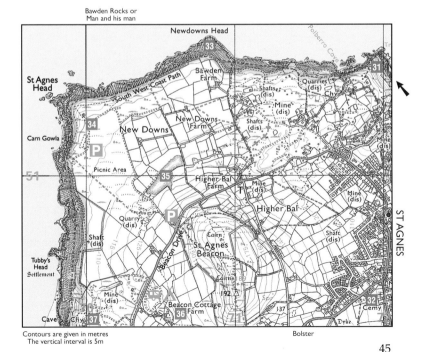

Contours are given in metres
The vertical interval is 5m

Bolster

South of Porthtowan, site of a short-lived smelter, the path is kept away from crumbling cliffs, following the perimeter fence of the airfield at Nancekuke. The steps down Sally's Bottom are made of distinctive Portuguese granite, quite different from the local granite.

Portreath Harbour **38** was once known as Basset's Cove, because the lords of the manor, the Bassets of Tehidy (see page 63), used it for recreation, and as well as installing their bathing machine and a cottage they also cut six baths in the rock for seawater bathing.

A daymark – 'The Pepperpot' – sits above the harbour, which was built by the Bassets in stages from 1760 after the original harbour on the west side of the bay was destroyed. Wagons loaded with ore would have been run down the incline **39**, built in 1838 as part of the Hayle Railway, to the harbour. On the north side of the harbour Groundwork Kerrier have set up information panels about the Portreath Poldice Plateway trail which is waymarked from the square to the south coast of Cornwall. There is also a display in the Waterfront Inn.

Portreath has a good range of shops, cafés, a post office, accommodation, and buses both to Camborne and Redruth, and in summer along the coast.

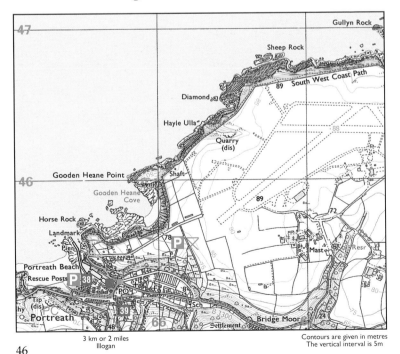

3 km or 2 miles
Illogan

Contours are given in metres
The vertical interval is 5m

Natural Arch
Cave

Chapel Porth
Chapel
(rems of)

Car Park

Natural Arch
Cave
PORT

Mulgram
Hill

Shafts
Shafts
Tip
(dis)
Shaft

NT

95

95

90

49

Mean Low Water
Mean High Water

Towan Rd.
Towan Farm

NT

Tip
(dis)
Shaft
Sandy Rd. 87

Porth Towan

Rescue Posts
PC
P
Shafts
Shafts
PO
Tip
(dis)
PH

Tip
(dis)

105

48

Adit

Shafts

Tips
(dis)
Shafts

Porthtowan
Shaft
Shaft
Chy
Tip
(dis)
Chy
Shafts

Tobban Horse

Tips
(dis)
Shafts
Shaft
Tips
(dis)
Chy
W Chy
Tip
(dis)

Adit
Shafts
Chy
Tip
(dis)
91

Shaft

Shaft
Shaft
Tip
(dis)

Shafts
Tip
(dis)

Sally's
Bottom
Shaft

Quarry
(dis)

Factory Farm
Tip
(dis)

Tips
(dis)

Porthtowan
Farm
Tel Ex

Shafts

Quarries
(disused)

Tips
(dis)

Mount Pleasant
Farm

88

Forthvean Road

Nancekuke Common

Tip
(dis)

96

Co Const & Co Bdy

103

Tip
(dis)
Shaft

Airfield
(disused)

Quarry
(dis)

87

School Farm

86

88

100

47

Museum

Southview
Farm

Tip
(dis)

Elm Farm

48

68

Lower Forge

Bridge

Mount Hawke
2 km or 1 mile

Contours are given in metres
The vertical interval is 5m

2 km or 1 mile
Bridge

47

A CIRCULAR WALK AROUND TREVELLAS COOMBE

$2\frac{1}{4}$ miles (3.6 km)

This walk at Trevellas Coombe, known locally as the Jericho Valley, will take you past many mining relics, but also past daffodils, at the right time of year, a malting house and a manor house, and a base for Spitfires. There is space here only to pick out a few features from the work done by the Cornwall Archaeological Unit, but you will see evidence of hundreds of years of tin-mining and smelting (see page 50).

Start from the car park above the beach at Trevellas Porth. Just above the beach are the remains of a 'blowing house', a medieval smelter where the blast of air was provided by bellows powered by water. As you look up the valley ahead of you, there is a breached wall with an adjacent pit, in which a water-wheel turned to work a set of stamps. The track going up the hill to the left is a sanding road, along which beach sand was carried to sweeten the acidic Cornish fields. The Coast Path is way-marked up this track, but for the circular walk you take the lower track, which is almost horizontal and is downhill of the chimney nearest to the beach. This chimney is part of a calciner and is typically Cornish, with the lower part built of stone with a few brick courses at the top. After you join the tarmacked road, you see on your left the solid base which supported the flywheel for a set of stamps and a winding engine. The surviving engine house held an engine that was used to pump water out of the Blue Hills mine. Its boiler-house chimney still stands.

Go through the gate and along the path above the cottage and sheds. Up to 1985 a living was made here by tin-streaming, concentrating tin from the sand and gravel then selling the high-grade concentrate to a smelter. Nowadays this is not viable but the owner does use the restored six-head of stamps, powered by the overshot water-wheel, to crush local ore, concentrate the tin and smelt it. You should be able to buy his small 2-ounce ingots of Cornish tin in St Agnes Museum **32**: 'Stean san agnes an guella stean en kernow', or 'St Agnes tin is the finest tin in Cornwall'. If you buy an ingot remember that it is St Agnes tin, not just Cornish tin.

Walk up through the valley, and above Jericho Cottage the path goes through a wood which may be full of daffodils now but was formerly the site of Jericho Stamps.

Do not cross the second footbridge **A** over the stream but take a sharp left, 'to Trevellas', up the hill. Just after you pass the cottage called Wheal Joy, thought to have been a malting-house, you will come to a tarmacked lane. Trevellas Manor Farm has obviously been much changed over the centuries.

At the junction take the road towards Cross Coombe but where the road turns sharp left, downhill, take the track alongside the airfield, built in such haste in 1941 that local farmers had little, if any, time to harvest their crops. At the coast turn left to Trevellas Porth.

Contours are given in metres
The vertical interval is 5m

49

Tin processing and smelting

In Trevellas Coombe, as in many other places in Cornwall, evidence for all the processes, from the mining of the ore to the production of tin metal, has been identified. 'Ore' is an economic term that refers here to the valuable mineral containing tin (cassiterite, tin oxide), plus all the valueless material, like quartz and slate, that has to be removed as well. Ore was broken up by hand, a job often done by women known as 'bal-maidens', and then was crushed by a set of stamps. These consisted of a set of hammers lifted by cams on a horizontal axle, which was rotated either by a beam engine or by water power. After being crushed by the falling hammers, the material was again separated, by devices such as round buddles, in which the lighter waste was

The remains of 20th century round buddles and other processing works at Cligga Wolfram and Tin Mine, which closed in 1945.

washed away, and then the concentrate was roasted in a burning house, or calciner, to release and drive off any sulphur and arsenic. The roast concentrate was then smelted to produce metallic tin, which was run off into moulds. Demonstration tours of a restored tin stamp and tin smelting are run by Blue Hills Tin Streaming.

When mining collapsed, because foreign mines could produce copper and tin more cheaply, the Cornish went to work in the metal mines of Australia, South Africa and the western side of the Americas, giving rise to the saying that 'at the bottom of every hole you'll find a Cornishman'.

Pilchards

Pilchards used to reach Land's End in enormous shoals in July, and then split so that some travelled along the north coast and some along the south coast of Cornwall. For about four months the huer, whose job it was to spot the shoal, kept a lookout from the cliff top for the silvery red roughening of the sea and the diving sea birds. When he spotted this he would shout 'hevva', meaning a shoal, down a long tin trumpet to the fishermen at sea, and by an elaborate system of semaphore would direct the boats to shoot the nets around the shoal, which was then towed inshore and the nets anchored. The next process was to 'tuck', or empty, the net. The fish were removed as needed to keep pace with the processing on shore in the pilchard palace. Here the fish were stacked between layers of salt to a height of about five feet and left for a month. Then the fish were packed in barrels with a weight on top to squeeze out the oil – this was sold separately. The fish were usually sold to Spain, France and Italy, and even today there is a firm exporting barrels of pilchards to Italy from The Pilchard Works in Newlyn.

Pilchard businesses were sold as 'seines', usually consisting of three boats, two nets and the fish cellars. Some idea of the scale of the industry can be gained from the fact that in 1870 there were 379 registered seines, 285 in St Ives alone, so each seine was allocated a time when it could net the fish. By 1920 the inshore pilchard fishery that had existed for centuries was dead.

Cornish fishermen had never chased just the pilchards, but had a year's work fishing for mackerel from Eddystone to the Wolf Rock from January to June, with herring in the North and Irish Seas being the quarry until the pilchard season started.

5 Portreath to St Ives

via Gwithian and Lelant
17¼ miles (27.8 km)

From the large car park above Portreath Beach follow the main
road across the bridge, then go up Battery Hill. Before the
continuation of the Battery Hill road **40** dives back to the beach,
there is a narrow track to the south of Western Hill. To get a
good view of Portreath and its difficult harbour climb up
Western Hill, which is owned by the National Trust, as is much
of the coast as far as Gwithian. The road often lies close to the
coast and the Trust has improved many of the areas where cars
can be parked, making access easy for people who wish to walk
only a short distance.

(For a complete contrast to the Coast Path you could leave the
coast **A** just south of Basset's Cove and take the circular walk
into the country park at Tehidy Woods (see page 61).)

Crane Castle **41**, an Iron Age cliff castle, most of which has
been eroded by the sea over the last 2,000 years, seems to be
oddly named, but it is thought originally to have been called 'ker
hen' or 'old fort'. At the east end of Derrick Cove the National
Trust has made a cliff viewing platform **42** for visitors in
wheelchairs. Further along is Hudder Cove, where at low tide in
1995 you could still see the remains of the *Secil Japan*, wrecked in
March 1989, with all but one of her crew saved by helicopter.
Hell's Mouth is a local tourist site, where a very short walk from
the road takes the less energetic to the top of a spectacular drop
to the beach, then back to the café, with water from the well for
the tea.

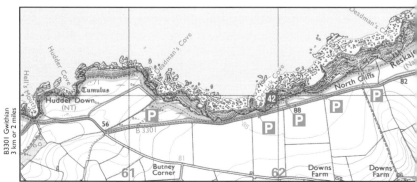

Contours are given in
The vertical interval

52

Gooden Heane Point

Gull Rock

Horse Rock
Landmark
Pier

Western Cove
Western Hill
The Horse
NT
Chy
40 Tip (dis)
PC
Portreath Beach
Rescue Posts
P
Portreath
48

Ralph's Cupboard

Porth-cadjack Cove
Carvannel Downs
Samphire Island
Carvannel Farm
Quarry (dis)
Tregea Manor
B 3301
83

Mirrose Well Cove
Spr
Chytodden Well
86

Basset's Cove
W
76
Penpraze
MS

Crane Islands
MLW
A
Mirrose Well
Trenoweth
Tehidy Barton
83
Tel Ex
P

41
MLW
P
Eastern Lod

Crane Castle
Path
2m
88
Earthwork
86

South West Coast Path
P
North Cliff Plantation
Tehindy Resr.
Golf Links
CH
90

Tehidy Country Park
Tehidy Woods
PC P
Tehidy Park

Hospital
Spr
Old Mer Farm

FB
FB
FB

Magor Plantation
Menwinnion
Oak Wood

Carvan Park
Magor Farm
54
Magor Plantation
South Tehidy
65
Halgoss

Illogan
2 km or 1 mile

ntours are given in metres
ne vertical interval is 5m

Tolvaddon Downs

53

Look out for grey seals as you walk out towards Navax Point. They use the caves below as breeding sites. Godrevy Island **43**, with its lighthouse, the inspiration for Virginia Woolf's *To the Lighthouse*, marks the landward end of a treacherous line of reefs, The Stones, which have claimed many wrecks. Perhaps the best known involved the loss of some of King Charles I's personal effects in 1646. His wife and his son, who became King Charles II at the Restoration, had fled separately to France via Pendennis Castle at Falmouth, which was then a royalist stronghold. The goods that came ashore were fought over on the beach by Bassets and Arundells, each claiming wrecking rights as lords of the manor. Apparently, although the goods landed within the Basset's territory they did not press their case, as they had supported the royalist cause, which by then was all but lost, even in Cornwall.

The beach of Gwithian is good for surfing and the area is full of chalets and holiday camps. The Red River **44**, which crosses the beach, once discharged thousands of tons a day of red iron oxide, residue from the tin mines, in its lifeless waters. The water also carried fine-grained cassiterite, lost from the mines' processing operations, and some of this was recovered by a series of tin-streaming works in the Red River valley. Much of the cassiterite reached the sea and was deposited on the sea bed, so that whenever the price of tin is high, plans are made to dredge it from the sea bed. Places like St Ives, which rely on tourists enjoying sandy beaches, object that the waste dumped back in the sea might pollute the beaches.

Beside the informal car park just before the 'settlements' **45** is that rarity on the Coast Path – a café that is open all year. The Godrevy Café, in a modern award-winning building, is open every day, except Christmas Day, from 10 a.m. to sunset, even if there is a gale.

Between Godrevy Towans and Green Lane evidence of habitation has been found from before the Bronze Age to the medieval period. Parts of the medieval village of Connerton have been excavated, although nothing is visible now except the round field **46** with earth banks, which was the pound in which stray animals were kept.

The path leaves Churchtown road along a lane and soon splits into many tracks, but you should be able to follow the acorn waymarks on posts as the Coast Path weaves through the sand dunes. An attempt has been made to mark out a sustainable route, but legally the Coast Path is still (in 1995) along the front

Nathaga
Rocks

Navax Point

43

Godrevy
Point

Mutton
Cove

Kynance Cove

Tumulus

SWC Path

The Knavocks
(NT)

△ 76

76

Castle Giver Cove

Fishing Cove

Godrevy Farm

National Trust

Homestead

Higher Pencobben

MS

73

67

P

The Cleaders

Manor House
(remains of)

Godrevy Rocks

NT

Godrevy Towans

Sand
Cot

P

Magow Rocks

44

Settlements

65

45

10

Quarry
(dis)

PH

PH

Gwithian Bridge

Mean Low Water

6

St Gothian's Chapel
(site of)

Reskajeage

Gwealavella

Gillick Rock

Mean High Water

12

Garrack

Quarry
(dis)

Co Const & CP Bdy

rap Rocks

SWC Path

PC

Churchtown Road

Green Lane

Cross

Nanterrow

Nano

P

Gwithian
Towans

Point

Gwithian

46

21

PH

Quarry
(dis)

Settlement

Shaft

Quarry
(dis)

Shaft
(dis)

32

Calize

Engew
Farm

Pennance

P

St Ives Lane

Godrevy
Cottage

59 Prosper Hill

Nanterrow
Cottage

47

Shaft

Pennance Vean

57

Lissadel

69

Nanterrow Lane

pton Towans

dit

Camping Site &
Caravan Park

Trevarnon
Round

80

Works

Earthwork

Trevarnon

Gwithian Road

Chy
Shaft

Treeve Farm

Cemetery

58

Pulsack Manor

59

Trevarnon Moor

60

Tumulus

Connerton

2 km or 1 mile
B3301 Venton League

Contours are given in metres
The vertical interval is 5m

↖ B3301 Porreath
8 km or 5 miles

55

of the dunes, which is why that impractical route is on the map. If the tide is low you might prefer to walk along the beach, but then you will miss a walking slalom. The banks and bunkers among the dunes were part of an explosives factory, once one of the largest in Britain, employing over 1,800 people; locally this area is called Dynamite Towans. Nowadays the dunes are better known for their diverse habitats and wildlife – 300 species of plant have been recorded, as well as many butterflies and moths, and glow-worms. Dunes are dynamic but they suffer from excessive trampling in summer and gales in winter, so major conservation work is being undertaken on many of Cornwall's dune systems, to preserve these habitats.

The path leaves the beach beyond the lifeguard's hut **B**, which is just to the east of where the rocky cliff starts again. The track then winds among chalets, passing spiny sea buckthorn bushes, until a car park is reached at the mouth of the Hayle Estuary. Some of the banks on the Lelant side have been

St Ives Bay from Godrevy Point.

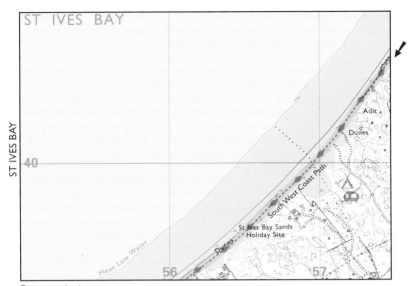

ST IVES BAY

ST IVES BAY

Adit

Dunes

South West Coast Path

St Ives Bay Sands
Holiday Site

Dunes

Mean Low Water

56   57

40

Contours are given in metres
The vertical interval is 5m

strengthened by a ship-breaker, with parts of a First World War destroyer. A ferry no longer makes the short crossing, but it is possible that the service will be reinstated. Without a ferry you have to walk to the old swing bridge **C** and then around Hayle Harbour by road, or catch a bus, if you wish to continue to St Ives.

If you want to continue walking, turn east from the 100-year-old swing bridge **C** at the entrance to Hayle Harbour. This is the oldest swing bridge with its machinery left in England, and is very wide, having been built for the Great Western Region's broad gauge. Follow the road along the inlet, under the viaduct and into Foundry Square, then under the viaduct again. Carnsew Pool **48** is a good place from which to view the centre of the estuary. To get there you need to take a footpath signposted to 'The Weir'. There is a path around Carnsew Pool, but you are asked not to disturb roosting birds. At the other end of The Causeway is the Old Quay House Inn **49**, which has a hide in its garden provided by the RSPB and for use by anyone. The RSPB owns the intertidal mudflats of the whole estuary. Up to August 1995, 250 species of bird had been recorded in the Hayle Estuary and some species, such as wigeon, teal and curlew, overwinter in numbers that are of national significance. Of course, when Birding South West (tel. 01891 884500) gives details of an extreme rarity, you are liable to see flocks of birdwatchers all looking at one American vagrant. In the old days such an exotic visitor would have been shot and stuffed.

Following the road further round the estuary, if you want to drop down to the shore you can take the minor road where the cross is built into the hedge **D**, but the official Coast Path continues along the main road to the Badger Inn, where the road turns towards St Ives but the path keeps to the lane leading to the church **50**. An alternative route can be taken by following the minor road to the east of the main road between **D** and **50**. St Michael's Way, a 12-mile (19.5 km) footpath to St Michael's Mount, starts here. There are two slate memorials inside the church and four old granite crosses in the churchyard. The bank round the churchyard is made of slag from the Copperhouse smelter.

The Coast Path now crosses the golf course, then passes under the railway bridge and along the dunes behind Porth Kidney Sands.

The path is well marked into St Ives (see page 60), but you can take a short diversion to St Uny's Well **51**.

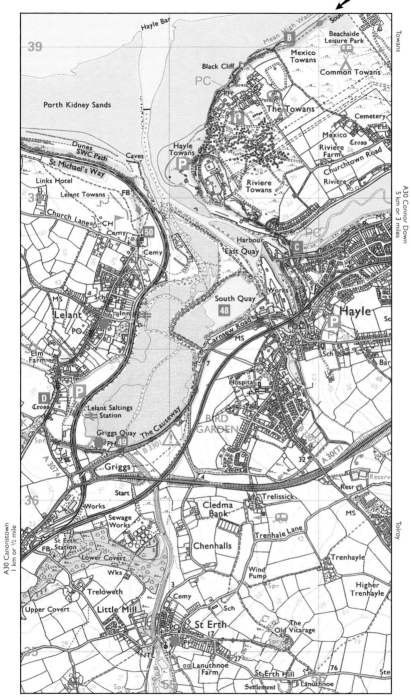

39

Hayle Bar

Mean High Water

South

B

Beachside
Leisure Park

Mexico
Towans

Common Towans

Black Cliff

PC

PH

The Towans

Cemetery

PH

Porth Kidney Sands

Mexico
Riviere
Farm

Cross

Churchtown Road

Hayle
Towans

P

Riviere

Dunes
SWC Path

Caves

Riviere
Towans

St Michael's Way

Links Hotel

38

Lelant Towans

FB

Church Lane

CH

Cemy

50

Cemy

Harbour

PC

MS

East Quay

C

Lelant

MS

Sch

Inn

South Quay

48

Works

Hayle

PO

P

P

PO

Sch

Bar

Carnsew Road

MS

Elm
Farm

37

7

D

P

Hospital

10

Cross

Lelant Saltings
Station

20

Griggs Quay

PH

49

The Causeway

BIRD
GARDEN

32

A 30(T)

Griggs

A 3074

B 3301

4

Resr

Reserv

36

Start

Trelissick

MS

Works

Cledma
Bank

Sewage
Works

Trenhale Lane

Chenhalls

Trenhayle

St Erth
Station

FB

Lower Covert

Wind
Pump

Spr

Higher
Trenhayle

Wks

Treloweth

Cemy

3

Sch

Upper Covert

Little Mill

PO

St Erth

17

The
Old Vicarage

35

NTL

PH

27

St Erth Hill

76

Ste

55

Lanuthnoe
Farm

Settlement

Lanuthnoe

Contours are given in metres
The vertical interval is 5m

St Ives

Nowadays St Ives is famous as a tourist resort and for the Tate Gallery St Ives which shows the work of the exceptional group of artists who came to work in the area. Names that are associated with St Ives include the potter Bernard Leach, the sculptor Barbara Hepworth and the painters Ben Nicholson, Roger Hilton, Peter Lanyon, Terry Frost and Patrick Heron, as well as the primitive painter Alfred Wallis. Work by Barbara Hepworth and others is scattered through the town: outside the TIC, in the library and church, and her studio and garden are open as an outpost of the Tate, so you can enjoy looking at semitropical vegetation through one of her pierced forms (or vice versa).

St Ives achieved earlier fame as the most important port for the pilchard fishery (see page 51), with its harbour, protected by Smeaton's Pier, full of boats and the town reeking of pilchards. Many objects from this industry, as well as much else, are kept in the museum which is well worth a visit.

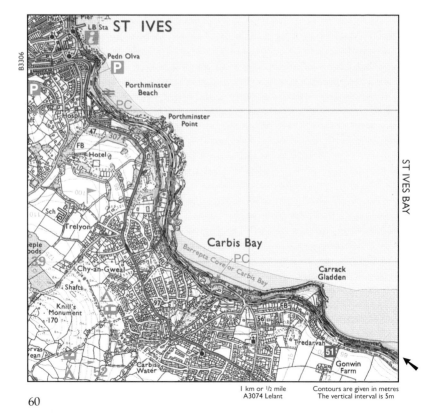

1 km or ½ mile
A3074 Lelant

Contours are given in metres
The vertical interval is 5m

A circular walk into Tehidy Woods

3 miles (4.8 km)

This is a short and easy walk with lots of variety, so it is suitable for children as young as four years old. If necessary you can take a shortcut along one of the signposted trails in this country park.

Leave the car at the National Trust car park at Basset's Cove **A** and head south on the Coast Path past Crane Castle **41**. Leave the Coast Path at the stile into the next field. Cross the road to enter Tehidy Country Park, owned by the county council, and continue through the second gate into the low, wind-pruned, mixed woodland. When the track divides take the path going downhill, but before the cottages turn downhill by the post with the arrows. At the Kennels Hill signpost turn down to Otter Bridge. There are no otters in the park nowadays. Take the path upstream (*no dogs, please*) and go round the lake, keeping to the path closest to the edge until you cross a bridge made of four granite slabs, where you turn downstream back to Otter Bridge.

Go back up the hill from Otter Bridge and take the path to East Lodge at the signpost. This leads under a range of larger, ornamental trees past the post-war buildings of the now closed Tehidy Hospital. Shortly afterwards you take a path identified with a red arrow leading off to the left. Follow this path until it appears to turn sharp left at a junction. Continuing straight on, you come out, across a narrow granite cattle grid, on to a grassy track alongside a field. At the road walk 50 yards (45 metres) to the left, then take the rough track back to Basset's Cove.

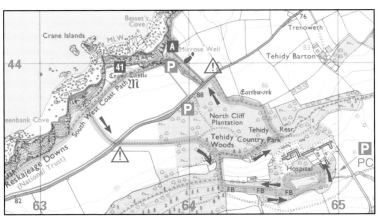

Contours are given in metres
The vertical interval is 5m

Harvey's, Trevithick and engines

Hayle used to consist of two quite separate industrial communities, Hayle to the west and Copperhouse to the east, whose intense rivalry as providers of machinery and materials for the mines led to violent intervention in each other's operations. Copperhouse was the scene of a short-lived attempt to smelt copper ore in Cornwall rather than taking the ore to the coal in the Swansea valley. Hayle was better known for its foundries, with Harvey's being not only pre-eminent but also the longest survivor. Harvey's made engines for metal and coal mines, for moving sewage (for example, one of the Kew Bridge Engines in

Inside the smaller of these engine-houses at Levant a Cornish engine, built by Harvey's in 1840, has been restored.

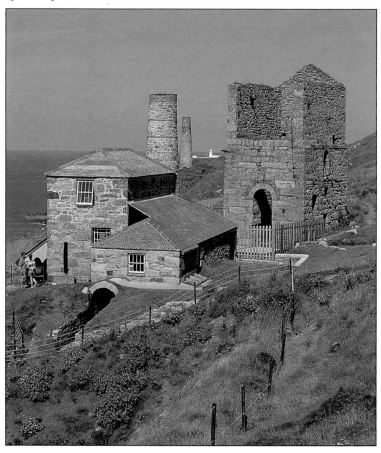

London), and for pumping water in Holland. It also built iron ships and the iron work for the Royal Albert Bridge across the Tamar, which Brunel built in 1859, and over which all the trains from Cornwall to the rest of England still travel. Harvey's engines could be found almost anywhere in the world to which Cornish miners had emigrated, and one is preserved locally at Levant Mine.

Associated with Harvey's were some notable engineers, of whom only Richard Trevithick (1771–1833) has received much acknowledgement. Trevithick, and others, advocated the use of high-pressure steam, at 65 pounds per square inch (psi) or more, rather than at only 2–3 psi, as in the Newcomen and Watt engines then in use. Trevithick also designed steam-powered vehicles, first testing these in Cornwall and giving rise to the locally well-known song 'Goin' up Camborne 'ill comin' down', before designing the world's first successful railway locomotive for the Penydarren ironworks in Wales in 1804. A full-scale, steam-working replica of this locomotive can be seen in the Welsh Industrial and Maritime Museum in Cardiff. However, most relics of Hayle's great industrial past seem to have been demolished over recent years.

The Bassets of Tehidy

Much of what you have been seeing in this area has connections with the Basset family, whose ancestors came across with William the Conqueror in 1066. They were the lords of the manor of Tehidy and owned the castle on Carn Brea, as well as most of the mineral rights in the area, making them one of the three or four most powerful families in Cornwall. Their wealth was vastly increased when the adit being driven to drain the mines around Carn Brea in the early 18th century struck rich copper lodes. The memorial on Carn Brea is to Lord de Dunstanville, a Basset, and Spratting Cove was renamed Basset's Cove after the original Basset Cove was developed by the Basset family as Portreath, from which they exported their ores. With the decline of the mines and a fondness for the horses, the fortunes of the Bassets had dwindled by the beginning of this century. In 1918 their manor house was sold to the people of Cornwall as a hospital.

6 St Ives to Zennor

via Clodgy Point
6½ miles (10.5 km)

This is a short but testing stretch, and half a day allows you plenty of time with St Ia's town, St Ives, at one end and the Mermaid of Zennor at the other. Since there is no accommodation, shops, pubs or cafés on the path between St Ives and Sennen, a distance of about 20 miles (32 km), it makes sense to book accommodation ahead at one of the villages off the path, and Zennor has much to recommend it.

From the harbour at St Ives you can cut through to Porthmeor Beach and pick up the path on Beach Road. However, the official route goes past Smeaton's Pier **52** and to the museum, and then round The Island, which is said to be the best place in Britain to watch the migration of sea birds. On the hilltop is a chapel dedicated to St Nicholas **53**, the patron saint of seafarers. This probably exhibited a light to guide fishermen before lighthouses were built. At the back of Porthmeor Beach is the Tate Gallery **54**, on the site of the old gasworks. The building, by

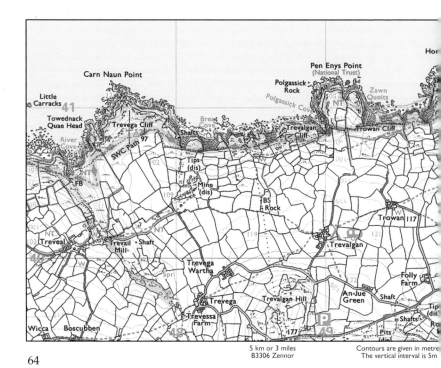

5 km or 3 miles
B3306 Zennor

Contours are given in metre
The vertical interval is 5m

Evans and Shalev, has won awards and even if you do not want to view the pictures and the pottery, you can get a free pass to walk past the stained glass window by Patrick Heron and upstairs to the bookshop and the excellent roof-top café/restaurant. Of course you could pay and see the work of artists who lived in the area and, indeed, how very diverse artists have seen the area through which you are walking.

Once on Beach Road, a waymark by the bowling green **A** shows that you are on the Coast Path, which is an easy walk as far as Clodgy Point (clodgy is Cornish for leper). From Clodgy Point all the way to Cape Cornwall the coastal strip is a site of special scientific interest (SSSI), and some is defined as an environmentally sensitive area (ESA). Roughly half of this coast is protected by the National Trust, including Hellesveor Cliff and Hor Point. The going is rough, as the track is uneven and boggy in places, although broken paving slabs and even a piece of boardwalk make for drier feet. The bogginess brings its own flora, including refreshing mint to chew and orchids to look at. Some streams have royal fern, fairly widespread in Cornwall but a rarity elsewhere in Britain. Near Polgassick Cove a badger sett and the path coincide, and it is common to see seals

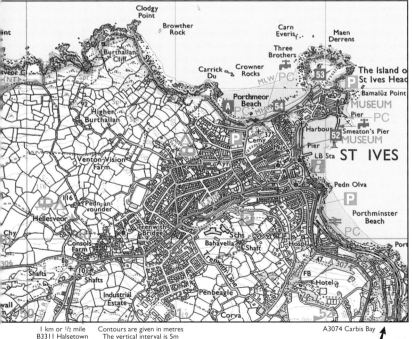

Zennor has a fine church and museum, a pub with a rock nearby from which John Wesley preached, a couple of farms . . . and a mermaid.

'bottling' or hauled out on rocks: The Carracks are a favourite spot.

There are a few mining relics and hundreds of little fields with the stones cleared to form boundaries. The fields date from the Bronze or Iron Ages and most are still being farmed. People tried to get food from the sea here, too, and boats were launched from Wicca Pool **55** and Porthzennor Cove **56**.

If you are intending to stop at Zennor, leave the Coast Path at a junction **B** on the west side of Zennor Head, and follow the track to the village. In the church the Mermaid of Zennor is carved on a bench-end. Legend says that she enticed a tenor in the choir down to Pendour Cove. By the church stands the pub and nearby is the Wayside Folk Museum. This houses artefacts gathered over the last 60 years, mostly from Zennor, and is open from Easter to the end of October.

Many people spend half a day walking to Zennor along the Coast Path from St Ives, then return by the Zennor church path across the fields. This path leaves Zennor between the churchyard and the village hall and links the hamlets of Tremedda, Tregerthen, Wicca, Trevega, Trevalgan and Trowan.

66

Penwith Environmentally Sensitive Area

Farmers in an ESA are invited to take part in the voluntary scheme and are paid a grant to farm traditionally, which among other things means maintaining existing field patterns and grazing rough land with cattle, but not using pesticides on it, or liming it or putting in new drains. The intention is not to create a museum, but to enable farmers to make a living in an area where the evidence for several thousand years of farming forms part of the landscape. The alternatives would be either dereliction or amalgamation of the tiny fields to make farms suitable for highly mechanised farming. In either case the landscape would change and the diversity of wildlife would decrease. The Penwith ESA includes about 17,000 acres (6,880 hectares) farmed by about 190 farmers, and agreements have been reached for about 94 per cent of the land.

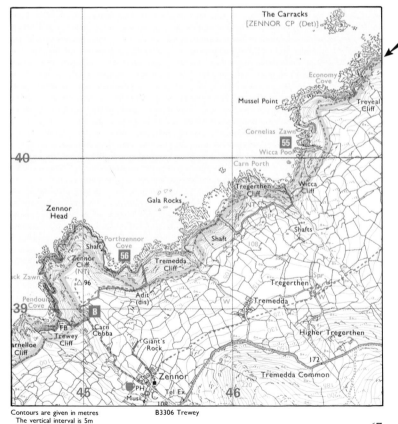

Contours are given in metres
The vertical interval is 5m

B3306 Trewey

7 Zennor to Cape Cornwall

passing Pendeen Watch and Botallack Head
10½ miles (17.1 km)

From the village at Zennor you take the track between the pub and the church and follow it to the west side of Zennor Head to join the Coast Path.

Pendour Cove **57** is also known as Mermaid Cove and, although you are unlikely to hear her singing, in the evening you might hear the badgers snuffling around by the sett beside the path. A little further on you can see the spectacular royal

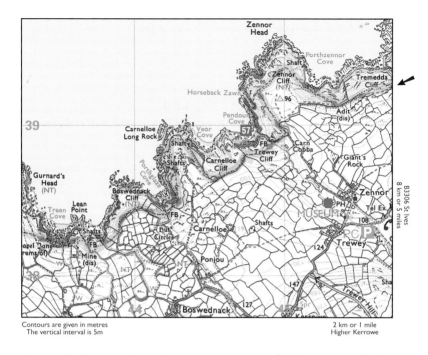

Contours are given in metres
The vertical interval is 5m

2 km or 1 mile
Higher Kerrowe

fern, which is nationally rare but occurs fairly commonly in Cornwall. Several orchids and bog asphodel are also found in these poorly drained areas.

Treen Cove, sheltered from the prevailing south-westerly winds by Gurnard's Head, was the site of both a pilchard seine (see page 51) and a more obvious tin mine above Lean Point. Gurnard's Head is supposed to bear a similarity to the fish, which most think ugly but which has a sculptural beauty, as well as being good stewed in cider or baked in foil. The headland is notable for its cliff castle and the remains of round houses and is now in the ownership of the National Trust.

On the west side of Porthmeor Cove **58** veins of light-coloured granite can be seen to cut through the original darker rock. The granite came in as a liquid several kilometres underground and can be seen only because the rock above has been eroded away over the last 280 million years.

Take care at Bosigran Cliff **A**, as many of the paths end at the top of sheer rock faces. These are suitable for either climbing up or abseiling down, and there are climbs here suitable for all levels of competence. If you are walking from the west you can often watch an ascent through binoculars as you approach, but beware of the sloping shaft right by the path **B**.

69

As you reach Portheras Cove **59** the signs of people not just coexisting with nature but trying to conquer it become stronger. The fields become larger, the houses more obvious, and there is more evidence of tin working. You are advised not to go on to the beach with bare feet because of sharp metal from the *Alacrity*, a coaster wrecked in 1963 and later blown up.

Pendeen House **60** was the birthplace of the great Cornish antiquarian William Borlase, whose comments on Cornwall in the 18th century are often quoted. In the farmyard behind the house is one of the largest fougous in Cornwall. These are underground chambers, but whether they were for storage or for ritual purposes is not known.

Pendeen Lighthouse **61** was opened in 1900 because passing

Contours are given in metres   B3306 Carnyorth
The vertical interval is 5m

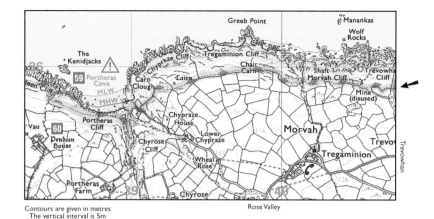

Contours are given in metres
The vertical interval is 5m

Rose Valley

vessels were unable to see either the Longships or Trevose Lights. Both could be hidden by high cliffs, and there were many wrecks, particularly on Gurnard's Head and on The Wra. In 1995 the lighthouse was automated in May, but was sometimes open to visitors later in the year. If you wish to visit, telephone Trinity House on 0171 480 6601 for up-to-date information. The village of Pendeen, along the road from the lighthouse, should meet most walkers' needs. The population is less than St Just's, inland from Cape Cornwall, but it is larger than any village on the route from St Ives. The reason for the size is Geevor Mine **62**, which took over the workings of the old Levant **63** and Botallack mines. Geevor Mine itself closed in 1990 and the area is no longer prosperous. As in previous closures many miners have emigrated, but a few retired men have found jobs – as guides at Geevor Tin Mine Heritage Centre. Back at the coast the indoor beam engine **64** at Levant Mine has been restored by members of the Trevithick Society and can be seen steaming. The engine was built by Harvey's of Hayle (see page 62) and was last used in 1930. It is the oldest surviving engine in Cornwall and is owned by the National Trust which has chosen the coastal strip from Pendeen to Cape Cornwall as the project for 1995, the Trust's Centenary Year.

Evidence of mining is found everywhere along this coast, but the most photographed relic must be the two engine houses **65** by the inclined Crowns Shaft of Botallack. These were restored by the Carn Brea Mining Society. The workings of Botallack stretched under the sea, and in Levant Mine not only could the miners hear boulders moving about on the sea bed over their heads, but after the mine closed the sea broke into the workings.

Two engine houses at Wheal Edward and Wheal Owles **66** have been restored as part of the NT's project. These mines produced tin and copper, with a little uranium, bismuth and arsenic.

At Kenidjack Castle **67** there is almost a surfeit of history. The engine houses were robbed to make the butts of the rifle range, and from the butts you can look down on a Bronze Age cairn. In the valley below there are the remains of many water-powered stamps for crushing the ores.

Cape Cornwall was thought in earlier days to be the most westerly point in England, but now that the crowds go to Land's End, it is relatively peaceful. The place is almost a microcosm of Cornwall, with fishing boats, mining remains, religious ruins and subtropical plants. And a new golf course.

Land's End Youth Hostel is in the Cot Valley, about 1 mile (1.5 km) down the coast from Cape Cornwall, and rather further from Land's End.

Cape Cornwall juts out into the sea with The Brisons beyond. Small fishing boats are launched from the safety of the beach in Priest's Cove.

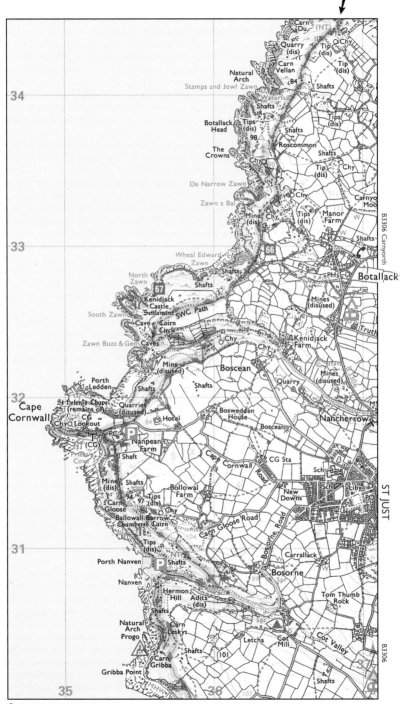

Contours are given in metres
The vertical interval is 5m

73

8 Cape Cornwall to Porthcurno

via Sennen Cove and Land's End
11½ miles (18.5 km)

Cape Cornwall, despite its grand name, is a low, little hummock compared with other mere 'heads' on this coast. The chimney **68** is a navigational mark and was said to have produced too fierce a draught for the tin mine on the south side of the cape, of which only the count-house (office) survives.

The Coast Path starts just below the car park, and when on top of the cliff you pass Ballowall Barrow **69**, a large and altered chambered cairn that was once buried under mine waste. The lush Cot Valley sometimes harbours rare birds blown across from America. After leaving the tin-streaming works at the end of Cot Valley, the path is well marked, but take care to follow the zigzag path **A** up the cliff, north of Gribba Point.

On the hill near Polpry Cove you can rest among several tumuli. The soil and the previous occupants have gone and the granite slabs make good seats. To the south lies Whitesand Bay, with the path running along the top of rapidly eroding low cliffs, before you are directed through palisaded dunes. If the tide is out and you wish to miss the sea holly and soft sand, it is more pleasant to walk along the beach. It is a popular one for swimming and surfing, but take notice of the lifeguards and any instructions or warnings. The village of Sennen Cove has a pub

The coast from Sennen Cove to Cape Cornwall.

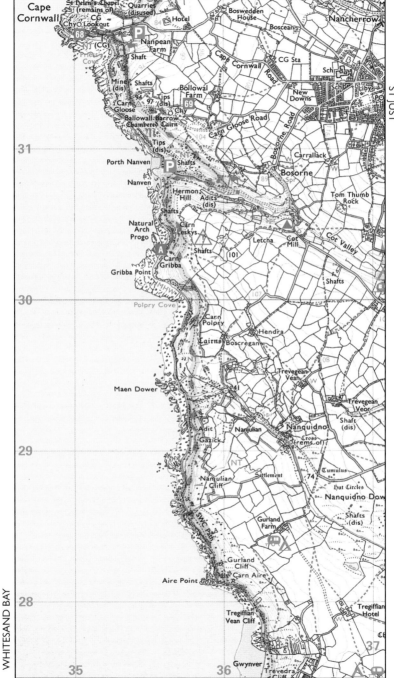

Cape Cornwall

St Helen's Chapel
(remains of)
Quarries
(disused)
Hotel
Boswedden House
Boscean
Nancherrow
CG Lookout
Chyo
68
P
Nanpean Farm
Shaft
Cape Cornwall Road
CG Sta
Sch
Prein Cove
Mine (dis)
Shafts
Bollowal Farm
New Downs
Sch
Lby
94
97
Tips (dis)
69
PO
Carn Gloose
Ballowall-Barrow Chambered Cairn
Carn Gloose Road
Bosorne Road
Carrallack
31
Tips (dis)
Shafts
Bosorne
Porth Nanven
P
Tom Thumb Rock
Nanven
Hermon Hill
Adits (dis)
Shafts
Natural Arch Progo
Carn Leskys
Letcha
Cot Mill
Cot Valley
A
Shafts
Carn Gribba
101
Shafts
Gribba Point
30
Polpry Cove
Carn Polpry
Cairns
Hendra
Boscregan
Maen Dower
241
Trevegean Vean
Trevegean Veor
Shaft (dis)
Adit
Nanjulian
Nanquidno
Gazick
Cross (rems.of)
29
Tumulus
74
Nanjulian Cliff
Settlement
Hut Circles
Nanquidno Dow
Shafts (dis)
SWC Path
Gurland Farm
Gurland Cliff
Carn Aire
Aire Point
Tregiffian Hotel
28
Tregiffian Vean Cliff
37
WHITESAND BAY
35
36
Gwynver
Trevedra Cliff
A
ST JUST

Contours are given in metres
The vertical interval is 5m

In summer the bright stems of the parasitic common dodder cover gorse beside a lichen-covered wall near Land's End.

cafés, a general store, car parks, a lifeboat station and the circular capstan house, which has been turned into a market. Behind the lifeboat station and the car park a pitched stone path continues up Mayon Cliff, leading to an easy, much trampled walk to Land's End. Take care if you are walking in misty weather, as many tracks lead to the cliff edge and waymarks are scarce.

Car parking is very expensive at Land's End, but the place has its uses for the walker in the form of public conveniences and refreshments. In summer the Royal Society for the Protection of Birds staffs the wildlife discovery centre, five days a week. West of Land's End is the Longships Lighthouse and 8 miles (13 km) SW is the Wolf Rock Lighthouse. The official Coast Path is waymarked again beyond Greeb Cottage **B**, but you will miss much if you follow the motorway-style track along the plateau.

Waymarks reappear at the north side of Mill Bay or Nanjizal **C**, where the path runs very close to the cliff edge. At the end of Nanjizal valley are the remains of a watermill. After this the path goes to Gwennap Head, named after an obscure Cornish

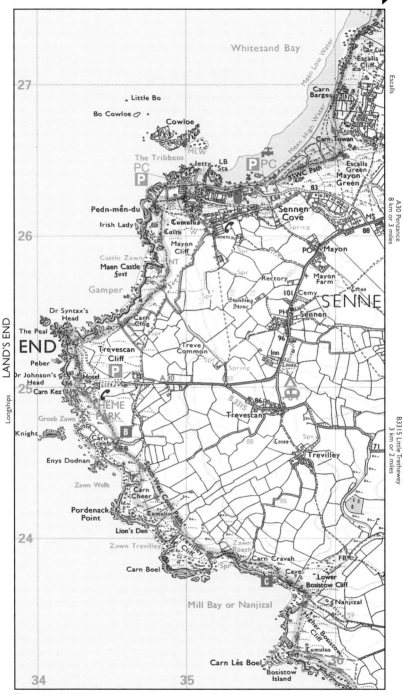

LAND'S END

Longships

Whitesand Bay

Little Bo

Bo Cowloe

Cowloe

The Tribbens

PC

P

Pedn-mên-du

Irish Lady

Tumulus

Cairn

Castle Zawn

Mayon
Cliff

Maen Castle
fort

Gamper

Dr Syntax's
Head

The Peal

END

Peber

Dr Johnson's
Head

Carn Kez

Greeb Zawn

Knight

Enys Dodnan

Zawn Wells

Pordenack
Point

Lion's Den

Zawn Trevilley

Carn Boel

Carn
Clog

Trevescan
Cliff

P

THEME
PARK

B

Carn
Greeb

FB

South West Coast Path

Carn
Cheer

Tumulus

Trevilley
Cliff

Carn Lês Boel

Escalls

Escalls
Cliff

Carn
Barges

Carn Towan

USWC Path

Escalls
Green

Mayon
Green

83

Sennen
Cove

MS

88

PO

Mayon

Rectory

Mayon
Farm

Standing
Stone

101

Cemy

Cross

SENNE

PH

Sennen

Treve
Common

96

Inn

Cross

Spring

A30

B3315

86

Trevescan

Cross

Spr

88

Trevilley

71

Cross

Spr

Zawn
Reeth

Carn Cravah

FB

Cave

Lower
Bosistow Cliff

Nanjizal

59

Mill Bay or Nanjizal

Higher Bosistow
Cliff

Tumulus

fort

Bosistow
Island

Escalls

A30 Penzance
8 km or 3 miles

B3315 Little Trethewey
3 km or 2 miles

Contours are given in metres
The vertical interval is 5m

77

saint. In 1995 plans were being made to reopen the lookout. The two daymarks help seamen locate the Runnel Stone, scene of many wrecks.

Offshore many birds and ships pass to and fro, and in spring and autumn and during south-westerly gales the area is full of birdwatchers, particularly above Hella Point **70**.

The path leaves Porthgwarra by a track in front of the cottages **D**, and not by the seaward track around Carn Scathe. Porth Chapel is a favourite beach, but access is strenuous, so it is less crowded than many. St Levan's Well is beside the path, but the hamlet of St Levan, with its church and a car park in a field, is a few minutes inland.

B3315 Trevecan
3 km or 2 miles

Runnel Stone

Contours are given in me
The vertical interval is 5

The Minack Theatre **71** was started in the 1930s. Its setting is similar to the Greek and Roman cliff theatres, but with its pseudo-Celtic designs in cement there is certainly nothing like it in the Mediterranean. A wide range of plays is performed daily in the season by mostly amateur groups; Kneehigh's inventive productions are in a different class.

Porthcurno is the landfall of a fibre optic cable laid in 1995 and of 14 now disused 'telegraph cables' (see page 129). The Trevithick Trust operate the Museum of Submarine Telegraphy in galleries in the granite. These galleries were cut during the Second World War to house the cable terminals. Porth Curno beach is composed of very coarse shell sand, and swimming here is very hazardous because of strong currents.

B3283 St Buryan
2 km or 1 mile

B3315 Treverdan
1 km or ½ mile

tours are given in metres
e vertical interval is 5m

9 Porthcurno to Penzance

through Mousehole and Newlyn
11 miles (17.7 km)

This is a superb coastal walk as far as the coastguard lookout at Penzer Point. From there until Penzance there are different attractions in Mousehole and Newlyn, with tedious road-walking between them. Except around Lamorna, the Coast Path mostly keeps to the cliff top, though there are steep drops into each cove.

The path leaves Porth Curno Beach up a steep track. Treryn Dinas is famous for the Logan Rock **72**, which is a large block of granite that could be rocked by pushing it gently, until

Contours are given in me
The vertical interval is 5

Lieutenant Goldsmith dislodged it in 1824. He was ordered by the Admiralty to replace it, at considerable cost in wages and beer, and it now rocks only with difficulty. Many people try to rock other blocks of granite. The path is routed outside the outer rampart **A** of the Iron Age cliff castle, and from here a path leads back to Treen.

Penberth Cove is much photographed and painted, because it is totally unspoilt. There are some boats, a capstan, a few cottages, and some very easily missed discreet public conveniences behind the National Trust sign. Porthguarnon **73** is even more unspoilt, while St Loy is almost tropical in its lushness. The path here goes along the back of the narrow beach **B** for about 50 yards (45 metres) and could be difficult with an onshore wind blowing and a high tide. From the land, Tater-du

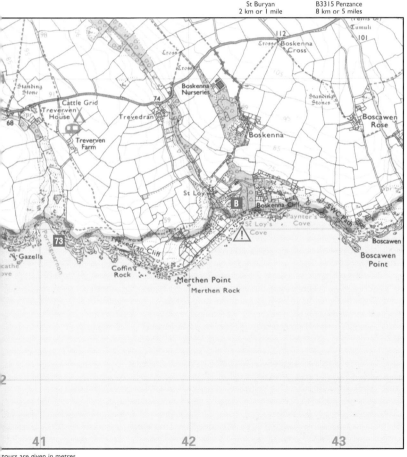

lighthouse **74** looks rather insignificant; it first operated in 1965 after this coast had witnessed more than the usual number of wrecks.

Lamorna Cove has several facilities: toilets, café, car park and, further inland, a well-known pub called the Lamorna Wink, originally an illegal beer house.

The old granite quarries here provided stone for the Café Monaco in Piccadilly, London, and for more challenging engineering works such as the Bishop Rock and the Wolf Rock lighthouses. The blocks were split by drilling a line of shallow holes, then by putting two wedges in each hole and hammering in a peg between them.

The tiny fields along this stretch of coast were used for early crops, particularly daffodils. Several disued bulbfields are now a coniferous wood **75** – a reserve owned by the Cornwall Wildlife Trust. The path goes through these trees and shortly after the disused coastguard lookout at Penzer Point it is routed above the bulb fields for the rest of the way into Mousehole (pronounced 'Mowzul', but named after the cave, The Mousehole).

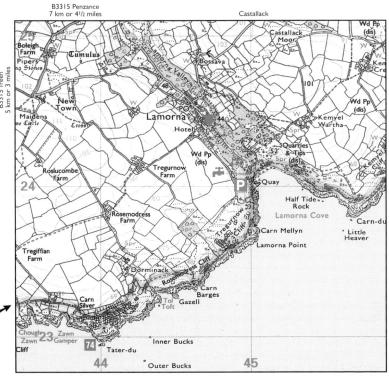

Contours are given in metres
The vertical interval is 5m

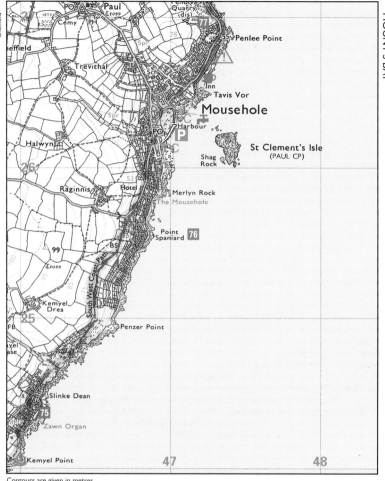

Contours are given in metres
The vertical interval is 5m

Point Spaniard **76** is reputed to be where the Spaniards landed in 1595, before destroying Mousehole, Newlyn, Paul and Penzance. It is traditionally believed that only one building in Mousehole survived their fires – the Keigwin. More recently, a large freezer-trawler, the *Conqueror*, landed on St Clement's Isle on Boxing Day 1977, but she slid off into deep water and can now be seen only by divers. A totally different Christmas tragedy in 1981 was the double loss of the Penlee lifeboat and the coaster *Union Star*, when a rescue attempt failed. Both crews, and the coaster's passengers, were lost. This is commemorated by a small garden at the lifeboat station **77**. The new larger lifeboat is stationed in Newlyn harbour.

Newlyn's medieval quay **78** is the oldest relic of what was, in 1995, the English port with the highest-value catch. If you are dismayed by the small range of fish available at your local fishmonger, you should look through the door at a fish auction, usually starting at 8.00 a.m., in the new fish market **80** built with financial aid from the EU. Much of the fish goes back to sea – on the Plymouth to Roscoff ferry – to be eaten on the Continent.

A short but worthwhile detour here, upstream just over the crossroads, brings you to The Pilchard Works **80**, the last vestige of the Cornish pilchard fishery (see page 51). In the 'works' you can not only see the process and sample a traditional cured pilchard but also learn how pilchards gave "meat, money and light, all in one night". The Coast Path does not go as far as the main road bridge, but crosses the stream by the Missions to Seamen building, before going down the lane passing seaward of the Newlyn Art Gallery.

Wherry Rocks used to have a tin mine on it, with power being transmitted by flat rods from the engine onshore. Battery Rocks

Small fishing boats tied up alongside Newlyn's medieval quay.

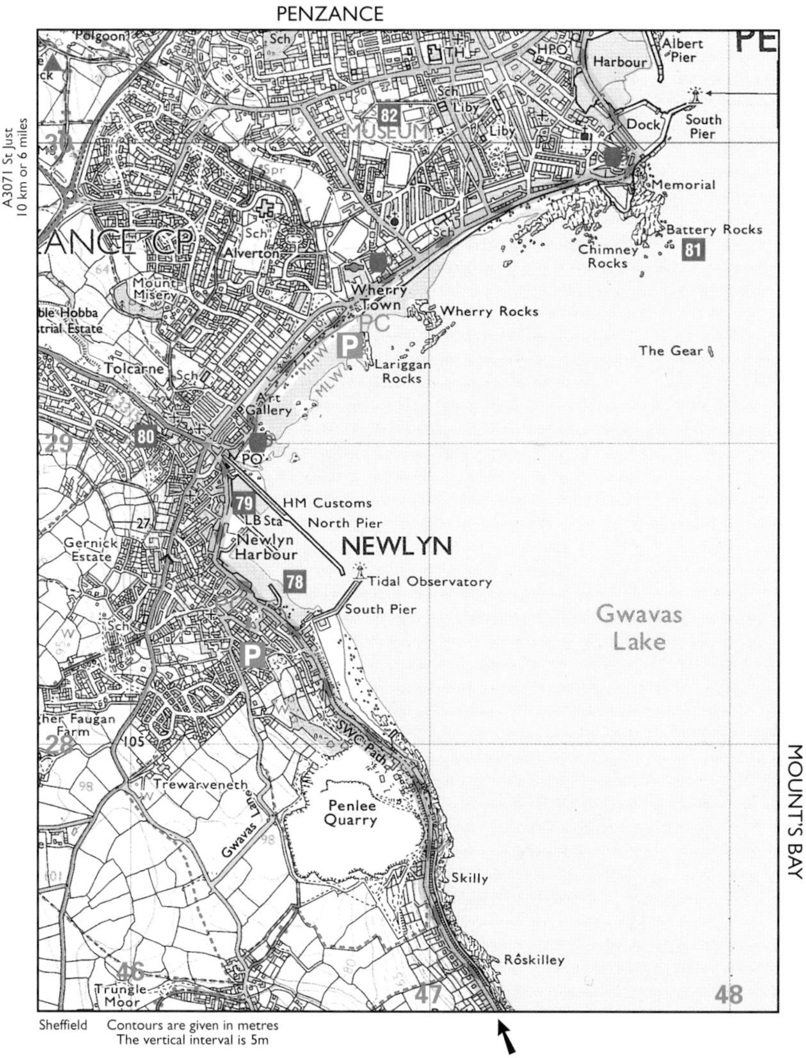

A3071 St Just
10 km or 6 miles

Polgoon
Sch
THC
HPO
Albert Pier
Harbour
PE
82 MUSEUM
Liby
Dock
South Pier
Memorial
ANCE CP
Sch
Alverton
Battery Rocks
Chimney Rocks
81
Mount Misery
Wherry Town
Wherry Rocks
ble Hobba
trial Estate
PC
Tolcarne
Sch
P
Lariggan Rocks
The Gear
Art Gallery
80
PO
29
79
HM Customs
North Pier
27
LB Sta
Gernick Estate
Newlyn Harbour
NEWLYN
78
Tidal Observatory
South Pier
Gwavas Lake
P
her Faugan Farm
28
105
Sch
Trewarveneth
98
Gwavas
Penlee Quarry
98
Skilly
101
Róskilley
46
47
48
Trungle Moor

MOUNT'S BAY

Sheffield   Contours are given in metres
The vertical interval is 5m

81 were just as their name suggests, with suitable guns for coastal defence. The main feature today is the restored Art Deco swimming pool, dating from 1935. Far older are the next buildings: the Barbican, the Dolphin, Coinagehall Street, the Trinity House building housing the National Lighthouse Museum, the Customs House and then Holman's dry dock. More of the district's history is in the excellent museum **82** in Penlee Park and in the nearby Cornwall Geological Museum.

The railway and bus stations, and the tourist information centre lie close together, at the base of Albert Pier.

A CIRCULAR WALK AROUND THE COAST AT TREEN
1½ miles (2.4 km)

This is a popular walk, which you can cover in only half an hour, but most turn it into a longer look at the cliffs, wildlife and the archaeological remains. Many people combine the walk with a visit to the pub in Treen. In summer a field is used as a car park, and out of season there should be no problem parking.

From the end of the road in Treen village, walk anticlockwise, so take the track that is signed as leading to Treen Cliff. At the coast you turn east and return to Treen up the very obvious path just inland of the rampart of the Iron Age cliff castle, Treryn Dinas. The coast here is owned by the National Trust and is a site of special scientific interest because of the rare plants lying among the western gorse, heather and bell heather of the heathland. The cliffs are granite, and weathering along the rock joints not only produces their typical castle-like appearance, but also the occasional logan stone. Such a rock **72** can be seen at Treryn Dinas (see page 80), if you follow the path out to the headland.

Contours are given in metres
The vertical interval is 5m

Plastics help the fishermen make a living in unspoilt Penberth Cove.

Penzance

Penzance is worth exploring. While cars rush by on one side of the town along the new road towards Land's End, walkers can easily rush by along the sea front, drawn by the obvious attraction of St Michael's Mount, but it is far better to call in at the tourist information centre near the railway station for a free town map, and then spend a few hours wandering around the town.

Penzance's visible history is barely 200 years old – no buildings are known to have survived the destruction of the town by the Spaniards in 1595 and most of the buildings around Market Jew Street, the main shopping area, date from the 18th century. The lower side of Market Jew has also seen more recent destruction, but the view up towards the elegant Market House, with the raised pavement, known as 'The Terrace', on the right, is still one of the finer pieces of townscape in Cornwall. In front of the Market House stands a statue of Humphry Davy, a local man and the greatest chemist of his day. Davy is most widely known as the inventor of the safety lamp, an invention that saved the lives of innumerable coal miners, who had previously used candles. These frequently ignited the fire-damp, chiefly methane gas, with disastrous results. Methane is generated by coal and is not found in Cornish metal mines.

Behind the Market House you can turn left into Chapel Street to see the extraordinary Egyptian House, built in 1835–36 and now used by the National Trust as a shop. If you retrace your steps to Alverton Street and then follow Morrab Road past the public library, with a Spanish cannon apparently trained on those who wish to enter, you will reach Penlee Park and the small Penlee Museum and Art Gallery. Small it may be, but the gallery has a very good collection of paintings by the Newlyn School of Painters (Stanhope Forbes, Lamorna Birch, Elizabeth Armstrong, Henry Scott Tuke, and others), and upstairs the museum has much to complement what the walker will have seen of the wildlife, geology, antiquities and mining. If you go back up Morrab Road you will come to the imposing old municipal buildings, which include the collections of the Royal Geological Society of Cornwall, the second oldest geological society in Britain, founded in 1814. Sir Humphry Davy was a vigorous supporter, and if the Society had adopted a proposal to sponsor a Professor of Mineralogy, Penzance might well have had a school of mines and even a university – an intriguing thought.

As it was, in 1663 the town had successfully petitioned to become a 'coinage town', testing the purity of all the tin ingots produced in the area, which would then be exported through the port. Formerly the tin had been assayed at Helston and shipped from Gweek. The harbour was also used for the fishing fleet, and Mousehole, Newlyn and Penzance vied for prominence over the centuries. They all suffered from 'Turkish' pirates (in reality slavers from the Barbary Coast of North Africa) who took men, women and children.

In the early 19th century Penzance, with its mild climate, was known as a resort for the gentry, who could not so easily visit the Continent because of hostilities. With the railway connection between Penzance and Paddington in 1866 came tourists and the development of hotels, so that today the port area seems almost divorced from the rest of the town.

Penzance still handles the boats to the Isle of Scilly, as well as having Holman's dry dock, but most of the fish is landed at Newlyn.

The new National Lighthouse Centre, on the waterfront in the old Trinity House building near the dry dock, has been created so that Penzance has a new tourist attraction.

Market Jew Street in Penzance is dominated by the market house. Much of the building is now a bank.

10 Penzance to Porthleven

passing St Michael's Mount and Praa Sands
13¼ *miles (21.3 km)*

This is an easy stretch and could be walked by anyone able to cross stiles and walk along a beach.

The route leaves Penzance railway and bus stations along the main road, but then a footbridge carries the path over the railway lines and on to the back of the beach. Marazion Marsh **83** is a well-known site for over-wintering aquatic birds, as well as being a major starling roost and a breeding site for the rare Cetti's warbler. A road follows the side of the open water in the marsh, so bird watching is simple. The Royal Society for the Protection of Birds organises guided bird watches in summer.

St Michael's Mount was a Benedictine Priory before it became a fortress in the 12th century, and later a major port for

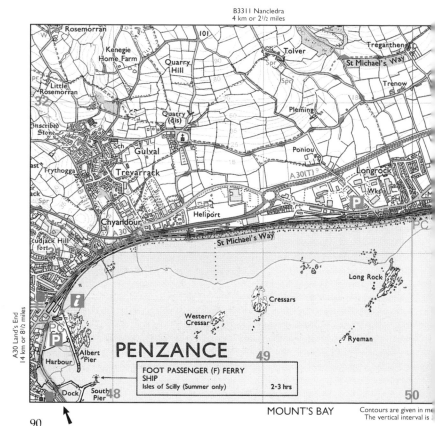

exporting tin and copper. Much of what you see was remodelled in Victorian times: more Neuschwanstein than military design. The real interest in the mount is its history before the Benedictines: was it Ictis, a tin-trading port of the first millenium BC mentioned by the Roman Diodorus? Nowadays the National Trust holds it for posterity.

Marazion is sometimes called Market Jew but originally these were separate places. Market Jew comes from the Cornish 'marghas yow' or 'Thursday market', and Marazion from 'marghas byghan' or 'little market'. Both had charters in the 11th century.

The Coast Path uses the road through Marazion until Henfor Terrace **A**, from where it returns to the beach for a very short stretch. This can be a problem with a high spring tide and a heavy sea, and if this is the case, an inland alternative would be to carry on along the road from Marazion and turn right by the cemetery to walk to Perranuthnoe, where you rejoin the route.

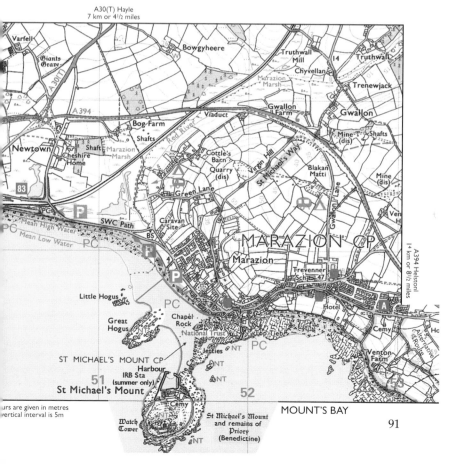

MOUNT'S BAY

At the time of writing (1999) the path has been diverted inland due to a cliff fall between Trenow Cove and Basore Point. The Coast Path wanders along the cliff top and through little fields to Cudden Point. Above the path lies the surprising Acton Castle Hotel **84**, built in the grand manner by an industrialist.

Prussia Cove **85** is named after the King of Prussia, alias John Carter, a notorious smuggler. The cove was originally called Porthleah Cove, but it became the base for the Carter family 'business', with the storage caves in Piskies Cove, and the harbour and the roadway from it in Bessy's Cove: the ruts across the beach bear witness to the scale of operations. On the cliff top was a small battery to discourage the revenue boats, and nearby was a kiddlywink selling liquor on which duty had not been paid. This was run by Bessy Bussow, in whose honour the cove is named.

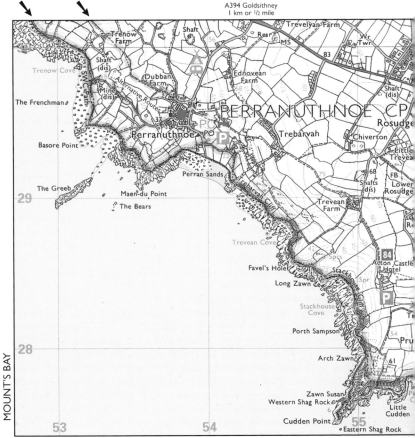

Contours are given in m
The vertical interval is

In 1947 HMS *Warspite*, *en route* to the breakers, was wrecked here, and the iron-bound post and chains between Piskies Cove and Bessy's Cove are relics of the salvage, carried out over six years here and at Marazion. She had broken free from her tugs near the Wolf Rock and was the largest wreck ever to occur on the Cornish coast. Her boilers still lie off St Michael's Mount.

Porth En Alls **86** is the base for the music masterclasses of the International Musicians' Seminar, followed by concerts in local churches.

Above Kennegy Sand the path crosses the dumps of the Speedwell tin and copper mine **87**, and you may be able to find amethyst among the waste.

If you are leaving Praa Sands, heading towards Penzance, you will find the path seaward of the bungalows **B** to the west of the pub on the beach (the Welloe Rock Inn).

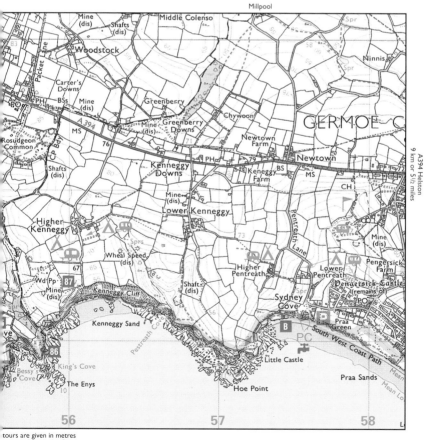

tours are given in metres
e vertical interval is 5m

Above Porthcew stands the Wheal Prosper engine house **88**, owned by the National Trust, while below on the beach and in the cliffs the contact line between the granite and the slate can be seen. More engine houses in dramatic positions are found at Trewavas Cliff, but most of the mining took place much further inland near, or on, Tregonning Hill.

Porth Sulinces lies not on granite but on slate, and this gives rise to a continual problem with landslips. For your own safety keep to the waymarked or fenced path and take notice of any cracks opening up in the ground.

Just east of Tregear Point there is a monument **89** to all drowned men, women and children who, prior to the Grylls Act

of 1808, were buried on the cliffs, rather than in consecrated ground. On the beach below is the Giant Rock, made of garnet-gneiss, and quite different from all the other rocks in Cornwall. How it got there is a matter for debate: was it pushed by a glacier or dropped by melting ice? It, and the area around it, is now protected as a site of special scientific interest.

Porthleven is a fishing village with a pleasant dockside. Many of its old buildings, some dating from the early 18th century, are still intact and put to modern uses. Most of the new building, mainly to house families connected with the Culdrose helicopter base, has been kept away from the old part of the village.

tours are given in metres
e vertical interval is 5m

Cornish place names

Near the River Tamar, the boundary between the counties of Devon and Cornwall, many of the place names are of English (i.e. Anglo-Saxon) origin, but further west Cornish takes the place of English, and by the time the Land's End peninsula is reached non-Cornish names are a rarity. Thus most of the place names encountered on this part of the coast are of Cornish origin, though both 'Padstow' and 'Falmouth' are English. The earliest name recorded for Padstow is 'Sancte Petroces Stow', the holy place of St Petroc (Pedrek), in 981, while the earliest references to 'Falemouth' and 'Fallmouth' date from the 15th century. Cornwall itself is 'Kernow' in Cornish, and is thought to originate from the name of a tribe called the Cornowii or 'horn-people', possibly because they lived at the end of the peninsula. Many places are self-evidently named after saints, for example St Ives (St Ia), but with many others the 'saint' has been dropped: examples are Zennor, Constantine, Gwithian, Paul, Gunwalloe and Gwennap. Various descriptive words are common in Cornish place names, for example:

als/alt	cliff
bal	mine
bean/vean	small
bos/bod	dwelling
bre	hill
carn	tor, rock, crag
carrek	rock
castel	fort, village
chi/chy	house, cottage
dhu	black
dinas	fort
dowr	water, stream
eglos	church
fenten/venton	spring
glas/las	grey-green
goeles/wollas	lower
goon/noon	down
gwartha/wartha	upper
gwin/gwidden	white
hen	old
heyl/hayle	estuary
kew/gew	hollow

lann	church site
los	grey
lyn	lake
maen	stone
meneth	hill
meur/veor	great, big
mor	sea
nans	valley
ogo/fougou	cave
penn/pen/pedn	head, end, top
poll/pol	pool, cove
pons	bridge
porth	cove, harbour
ros	moorland, promontory
rys/rid	ford
sawn/zawn	cleft, gully
sten	tin
tewynn/towan	sand dunes
tir/tyr	land
tre(v)	farmstead, hamlet
treth	beach
wheal	mine
ynys/enys	island

During this century there has been a revival in the Cornish language, and it is possible to learn it at evening classes and even in some schools. In many churches the Lord's Prayer, beginning 'Agan tas-ny, us yn nef . . .', hangs on the wall, and in a few churches occasional services are conducted in the language. But this revival does not alter the fact that the language is no longer in use. The last native Cornish speaker is reputed to have been Dolly Pentreath, a 'jowster' or fish hawker of Mousehole, who died in 1777, although at Zennor there is a memorial to John Davey, reputedly the last person with any traditional knowledge of Cornish, who died in 1891. Certainly 1800 is accepted as about the latest date at which Cornish was in use by anyone as a living language, after a decline dating back to the first incursions of the Anglo-Saxons across the Tamar, probably in the 8th century. Dolly Pentreath, and others, acquired a late fame and a little cash for their knowledge of Cornish but, sadly, the only piece of her fishwifely repertoire that was recorded was 'Cronnack an hagar dhu', 'the ugly black toad', hurled at the squire who had upset her basket of fish.

11 Porthleven to Lizard

through Polurrian Cove
13½ miles (21.7 km)

This section is generally easy walking on the top of the cliffs, with a few steep-sided coves to cross. The main hazard is likely to be stiles made of serpentine, which walkers' boots polish and which become treacherous when they are wet.

The path leaves Porthleven by the castellated town council building with its clock tower, and uses the lane through the village until the car park at the entrance to the Penrose Estate, owned by the National Trust. (If you are coming from the Lizard and heading for Porthleven, leave the beach by the rough road at the start of the cliffs **A** and do not take short cuts: the old, direct route has fallen away.) The Loe **90** ('loe' is a Cornish word for pool) is the largest natural body of fresh water in Cornwall but has been in existence only since the 13th century when the formation of Loe Bar ended Helston's days as a port.

Swimming on either side of the bar is not recommended. The Loe receives water rich in phosphate and nitrate and so suffers from periodic blooms of toxin-producing blue-green algae, while the sea usually has a strong undertow. It is far better to keep your feet dry and to enjoy the sea holly, the rare yellow horned poppy and other plants rooted among the inhospitable gravel. Legend has it that the bar was formed when the giant Tregeagle dropped some sand from a sack that he was carrying. Tregeagle was a 17th-century inhuman land steward of the Robartes family from Lanhydrock near Bodmin. He was said to have been summoned from the dead to be a witness in a court case, but could not be returned to the dead and so was given impossible tasks, such as removing all the sand from a particularly sandy cove. Another legend with chronological problems has Excalibur, King Arthur's sword, being thrown into The Loe.

Above the bar is a memorial **91** to the 100 or so people who were drowned, and buried in the fields, after HMS *Anson* was beached in a storm in 1807. The local people were powerless to help and a young cabinet-maker called Henry Trengrouse resolved to design a system that might have saved their lives. In 1808 he invented a rocket with a line attached that could be fired from either a ship or the shore. At great personal cost his breeches buoy system was adopted, and he died penniless in 1854. The grateful government had awarded him £20.

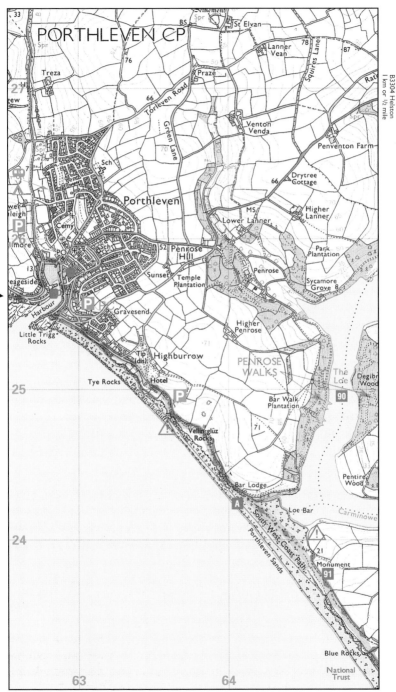

Contours are given in metres
The vertical interval is 5m

The yellow horned poppy, with its long sickle-shaped seed pods, grows among the flinty gravel on the top of Loe Bar.

Further along, one of the windlasses **92** possibly came from the 1890 wreck of the *Brankelow*. The cliff is slipping here so you need to heed any re-routing of the path and follow the waymarks, while above Halzephron ('cliff of hell') Cove even the road has slipped and been re-routed, leaving a temporary car park.

Winnianton **93** was a Saxon royal manor and figures large in *Domesday*, but today visitors come seeking the tranquillity of Gunwalloe Church, and maybe to look for gold coins from the Spanish and Dutch wrecks on this storm-battered coast.

To the south of the large hotel, now a retirement home, above Poldhu Cove is the remains of Marconi's wireless station **94**, from where the first transatlantic radio message was sent in 1901 (see page 128). The next cove south is Polurrian Cove, and from either the cove or the large hotel above it a short walk leads into Mullion with its church with 16th-century carved bench-ends. Mullion Cove is 2 miles (3.2 km) from the centre of Mullion and there is a good view from the car park in front of the large hotel on the north side: useful for disabled people.

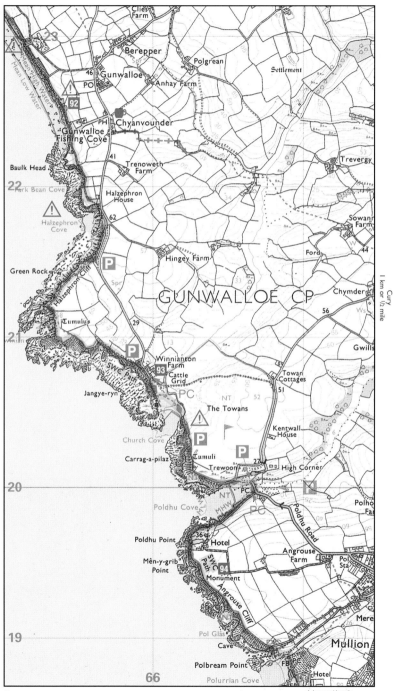

Clies Farm
Berepper
Polgrean
Settlement
Gunwalloe
46
PO
Anhay Farm
92
PH
Chyanvounder
Gunwalloe Fishing Cove
Mean Low Water
Baulk Head
41
Trenoweth Farm
22
Park Bean Cove
Halzephron House
Halzephron Cove
62
Hingey Farm
P
Green Rock
Halzephron Cliff
Spr
Ford
44
Sowan Farm
W
GUNWALLOE CP
Chymder
Tumulus
29
56
Gwills
21
P
Winnianton Farm
Towan Cottages
51
SWC Path
93
Cattle Grid
Jangye-ryn
PC
The Towans
NT
52
Kentwall House
Church Cove
P
Carrag-a-pilaz
Tumuli
Trewoon
High Corner
27
20
Poldhu Cove
PC
NT
MHW
PC
Poldhu Road
Polho Fa
Poldhu Point
36
Hotel
Angrouse Farm
Mên-y-grib Point
SWC Path
94
Monument
Pol Sta
Angrouse Cliff
Mere
19
Pol Glas
Cave
Mullion
Polbream Point
FB
Hotel
66
Polurrian Cove

Cury
1 km or ½ mile

Contours are given in metres
The vertical interval is 5m

1 km or ½ mile
B3296 Mullion Cove

101

Mullion Island, made of lava that erupted on the sea bed around 350 million years ago, is the most important nesting site for birds on the Lizard; cormorants, shags, kittiwakes and black-backed gulls are the main tenants. South of Mullion is a national nature reserve **95** managed by English Nature, and inland the Cornwall Wildlife Trust has a reserve of 99 acres (40 hectares) of heathland on Higher Predannack Downs, north of Predannack Airfield. The airfield is used mostly for helicopter training, and the partially dismembered corpses of aircraft visible from the Coast Path are kept for firefighting and for practising removal of people from crashed planes.

Gew-graze **96** makes a sheltered spot to stop, as the path drops from the flat downs into the valley. Soapstone was quarried here and sent to the potteries before the Cornish china clay industry began. Back on the downs, the twin towers of the Lizard lighthouse come into view before the path drops into

Mullion Cove has always been a base for fishing, but in the past wrecking and smuggling were probably more profitable along this coast.

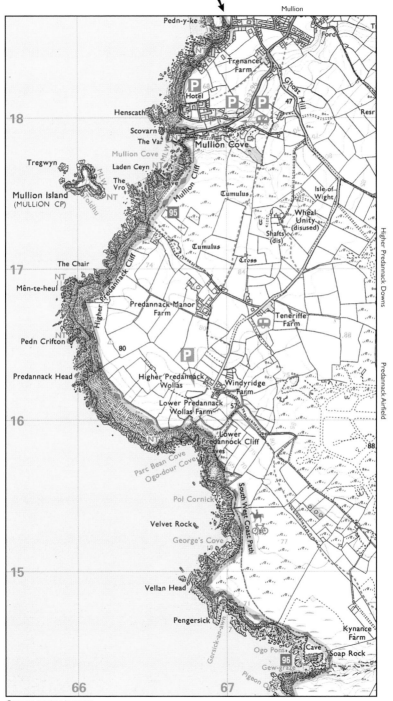

Mullion

Pedn-y-ke

Trenance
Farm

Ghost Hill

Hotel

47

Resr

Henscath

Scovarn
The Var

Mullion Cove

Mullion Cove

Tregwyn

Laden Ceyn

The
Vro

Cave

Mullion Cliff

Tumulus

Isle of
Wight

Mullion Island
(MULLION CP)

95

Wheal
Unity
(disused)

Shafts
(dis)

Cumulus

Cross

The Chair

Mên-te-heul

Higher Predannack Cliff

74

84

Predannack Manor
Farm

Teneriffe
Farm

Pedn Crifton

80

88

Predannack Head

80

Higher Predannack
Wollas

Windyridge
Farm

75

Lower Predannack
Wollas Farm

57

Lower
Predannack Cliff

88

Caves

Parc Bean Cove

Ogo-dour Cove

70

Pol Cornick

South West Coast Path

Velvet Rock

George's Cove

77

Vellan Head

71

Pengersick

Kynance
Farm

Ogo Pons

Cave

Soap Rock

96

Gew-graze

Pigeon Q

Higher Predannack Downs

Predannack Airfield

66

67

Contours are given in metres
The vertical interval is 5m

103

Kynance Cove **97**. Apart from the privately owned seasonal café most of this popular area is managed by English Nature and the National Trust. Cars are kept up on the downs and visitors who arrive at the car park are actively discouraged from trampling the rare Lizard flora. If walkers use the new made-up paths from the car park for a couple of hundred yards, instead of the Coast Path, the process of regeneration will be aided. The NT's work here has even won a Europa Nostra award. The islands and beaches are accessible at low water, but there is a great risk of being cut off as the tide rises. Wild asparagus is found on Asparagus Island, and the two sheltered valleys leading to the

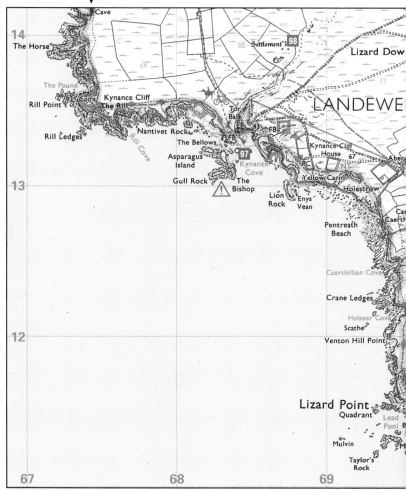

Contours are given in m
The vertical interval is

cove contain a wealth of the special flora of the Lizard, such as bloody cranesbill and thyme broomrape. The settlement **98** dates from the Bronze and Iron Ages.

Lizard Point, called Lizard Head on all old maps, is the western side of the headland. To the east, where the road from Lizard town ends, are cafés and a plaque with the service record of the Lizard lifeboats, while down in exposed Polpeor Cove is the disused lifeboat station **99**. The most southerly point is Bumble Rock to the east. The lighthouse was built in 1751 and is due to be automated in 1997: it should be possible to visit until the conversion works starts (contact Trinity House tel. 0171 480 6601). Both towers used to exhibit a light to distinguish the Lizard from Scilly's one light and the three lights of Le Casquet in Jersey. Nowadays sailors recognise lights by the pattern, duration and colour of their flashes.

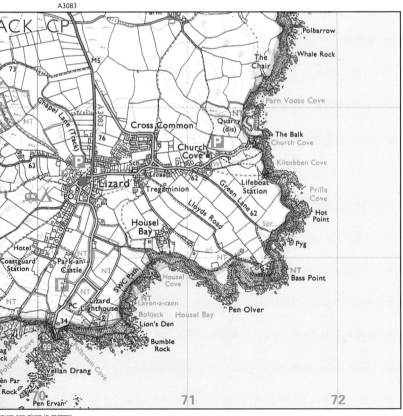

cours are given in metres
e vertical interval is 5m

A circular walk around the Lizard
4¼ miles (6.8 km)

Park in the centre of the Lizard town and take the road between the green (i.e. the car park) and the public conveniences. Carry on along the unmade-up lane, with cultivated fertile soils on schists to the left of you, and houses and heathland on infertile serpentine to the right. After the last house, continue down the footpath into Caerthillian Cove, where you join the Coast Path leading towards Lizard Point, the western side of the headland, then on to Church Cove **101**. There is a disused lifeboat station **99** in Polpeor Cove, and to the east the twin-towered lighthouse.

At Bass Point are Lloyd's Signal Station **100**, a daymark, and a coastguard lookout, now manned by Coastwatch. Notice the invasive Hottentot fig plants.

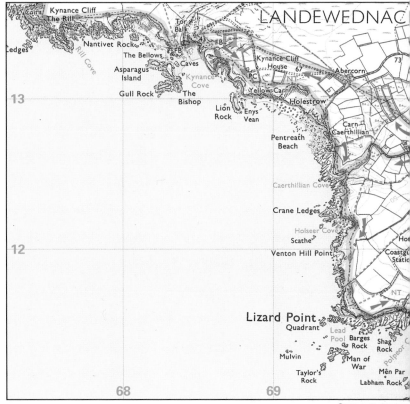

Contours are given in m
The vertical interval is

At Church Cove **101** leave the Coast Path and return up the track, which becomes a metalled road past the workshop of a serpentine turner. Further up is Landewednack Church **102** (Church Cove village on the map), dedicated to St Wynwallow. The present church, the most southerly in Britain, has a few remaining Norman features. The serpentine and granite tower and the font both date from the 15th century, and the pulpit dates from a Victorian restoration. From the church, walk up the road, past the old cross, to the village green.

Kynance Cove could be included in a longer alternative walk, but it is easy to miss the path where it leaves the lane about 100 yards (90 metres) beyond the public conveniences. The path lies on top of the double hedge, and to reach it you climb up steps beside the block-built bungalow that sits on an unfenced triangular plot to the right of the lane. Walk along the top of the double hedge, and over the fields to Abercorn. Here you join the road to Kynance car park for a few yards, and then head out across the heath by the bungalow called Carn Goon, later to join the path down into Kynance from the bottom of the National Trust's car park. From here head eastwards past Pentreath Beach to join the main circular walk by Caerthillian Cove.

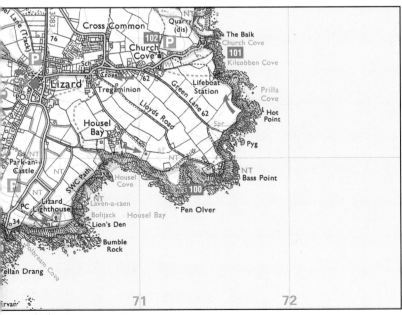

The Lizard

The Lizard is unique. This uniqueness arises mainly from the geology, but also from the mild oceanic climate and the flatness of the land. Currently most geologists think the Lizard is an 'ophiolite', a piece of ocean floor which has been thrust up. The Lizard is famous for its serpentine, which is thought to be a slightly altered slab of the Earth's mantle, the zone between the crust and the molten core. On the poorly drained plateau that makes up most of the Lizard, this rock produces poor, thin soils rich in magnesium. On these grow Cornish heath, western gorse, bell heather and some rarities, with a distinctive set of plants including more rarities on the salt-sprayed clifftop heathland. The jumbled mass of colourfully streaked rock on the coast gives rise to such long-standing tourist attractions as Kynance Cove.

The rock is also the source material for the Lizard's cottage industry of making turned stone ornaments, but in the industry's fashionable Victorian heyday what can only be des-

The cliffs of serpentine, schist and gneiss on the east side of the Lizard from Church Cove to Lankidden.

cribed as a factory developed at Poltesco, with an export business and a London office.

The other rocks on the Lizard include schist and gneiss, formed under very high pressures and temperatures within the Earth. These give rise to better soils with a quite different natural flora, as well as very abrupt changes in land use where they are in contact with the serpentine. Naturalists know the Lizard not only for its flowers, but also for some rare insects and the major breeding colonies of sea birds on the cliffs.

English Nature has designated many parts of the Lizard as sites of special scientific interest (SSSI), and large areas are included in the Lizard National Nature Reserve. The National Trust owns much of the coast and has covenants on further stretches, and both EN and the NT manage their areas for conservation. Since it is truly an unique area, one can only hope that with these safeguards it is protected from any further damage by insensitive tourism, farming and neglect.

12 Lizard to Coverack

via Cadgwith
11 miles (17.7 km)

The route is easy as far as Cadgwith, but from there to Coverack there are a few tiring climbs and steep slippery slabs of rock to cross. This really is the geological walk par excellence.

The route starts from the cafés and serpentine shop above the old lifeboat station **99** in Polpeor Cove. The rock collector can easily obtain most varieties of serpentine from the shop's waste, although the serious geologist will want to see the varieties *in situ* and will need a proper geological guide to the area. In Polpeor Cove by the old lifeboat house you will find gneiss, but the Coast Path is on schist, as you pass south of the most southerly house, past Housel Bay, to Church Cove.

The slopes of Bass Point are covered with Hottentot fig, regarded as an unwelcome alien, because the mass of stems chokes the native flora. The inside of the ripe fruit is edible – but please do not spread the seed or pieces of stem. On top of Bass Point stand not only a coastguard lookout, now manned by Coastwatch, but also Lloyd's Signal Station **100**, from where incoming ships were given visual orders about their future movements (see page 129).

In 1961 the lifeboat was moved from Polpeor Cove to the more sheltered station in Kilcobben Cove, which can be visited. Church Cove **101** has not only an old capstan house but also a fish palace converted into a restaurant. A worthwhile diversion here is to follow the route of the circular walk (see page 106) as far as St Wynwallow's Church **102** at Landewednack (Church Cove village on the map). This has a Norman door, though most of the church dates from the 14th to 15th centuries. St Guénolé (St Samson) was abbot of Landevennac in Brittany, and Gunwalloe Church is also dedicated to him.

The serpentine quarries to the north of Church Cove provided stone for the runways at Culdrose airfield, and crushed serpentine has also been used for firebricks.

Further on, the rock underfoot is schist, a black sparkling rock with fine white layers, which has been quarried above Chough's Ogo **103**, leaving a very comfortable resting place on the rock, but sadly there have been no choughs to watch here for the last 150 years. Further on a wooden seat has been provided, so that you can sit and look down into Hugga Driggee, more commonly known nowadays by its very fanciful English name of the Devil's Frying-Pan, a funnel-shaped depression with a natural arch at the bottom. The Coast Path winds through a private garden, then turns right to pass on the seaward side of the cottages. Cadgwith is many people's idea of a proper Cornish fishing village. It lost its lifeboat when the new lifeboat station was built at Kilcobben, taking the place of both the Cadgwith and the Lizard boats. On the north side of Cadgwith Cove the small hut with the chimney was a coastguard lookout.

A3083 Helston
15 km or 9½ miles

Ruan Minor
1 km or ½ mile

Contours are given in metres
The vertical interval is 5m

The slopes above Kildown Cove **104** are, like Predannack, the site of an experiment by the National Trust and a local farmer to stop the normal reversion of the fenced-off coastal land to scrub. A strip of coast has been boxed off by fences, gates built for walkers to open and close, the scrub cleared, and Shetland ponies used to control regrowth. Grassland rich in wild flowers is reappearing.

Poltesco is the site of an old serpentine works, from where the pulpit in Landewednack Church came. The water-powered serpentine factory took over the site from a pilchard seine (see page 51), which had built the rounded building as a capstan house for hauling in boats and nets.

Contours are given in metres
The vertical interval is 5m

Kennack Sands is a popular beach, with many caravan sites nearby, as well as beach cafés, a car park and public conveniences. Geologically the south end is interesting because of its complexity: the enigmatic Kennack gneiss, serpentine and gabbro, all within a few yards of each other. There are veins of asbestos here, and also veins of talc **105**, though not enough for a local cottage industry to produce Lizard talcum powder.

On the east side of Kennack Sands, after the concrete bridge, the path follows a lane seaward of the trees. It goes through an area of butcher's broom, growing on the alkaline soil, and on to Lankidden, with its tiny sandy beach and a track to the road, which could be useful for anyone who wished to miss the steep climb and descent at Downas Cove.

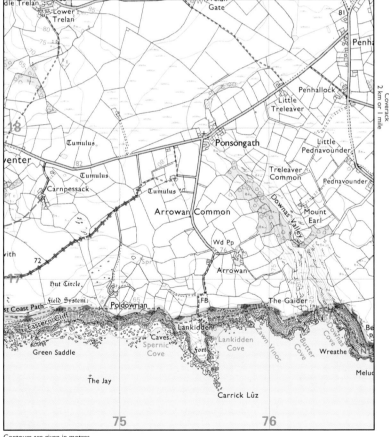

Contours are given in metres
The vertical interval is 5m

On a clear day it is obvious why a coastguard lookout was placed at Black Head **106**, as walkers from the Lizard can see Falmouth, the Dodman, and more headlands beyond.

Above Chynhalls Cliff there is a pig farm whose concrete yard continues across the path. The path then turns inland and returns towards the coast at the converted 'hotel', with a spur running out to the 'fort' at Chynhalls Point. The main Coast Path goes down seaward of the Wesleyan Chapel, and then hugs the coast round Dolor Point and the Paris Hotel, going past the old lifeboat station to the small harbour. Coverack boasts a youth hostel, cafés, shops, post office, excellent ice-cream (at the sign of the dancing cow!), a bus service to Helston, and an exposure of the Moho (the Earth's mantle/crust boundary).

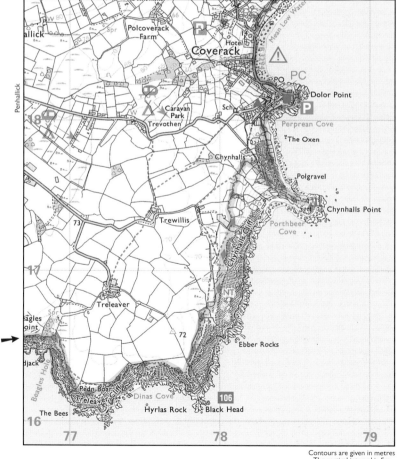

Contours are given in metres
The vertical interval is 5m

Squeezed into its narrow cove and valley, Cadgwith is protected from all but south-easterly gales.

13 Coverack to Falmouth

via Porthallow and Helford
22¼ miles (35.8 km)

This is a longer stretch than the previous chapters, and you may wish to split it in two, especially if the tide is wrong and you have to walk around Gillan Creek. However, the section from the Helford River to Falmouth is an easy one.

From Coverack's small harbour the path follows the road around the back of the beach, then goes along the lane between the houses, until a footpath leaves this lane just before the sewage treatment works. Follow this footpath and descend towards the beach. The flat expanse of ground behind Lowland Point, finally backed by a steep slope, is a good place to convince doubters that our present sea level is only transitory. During an

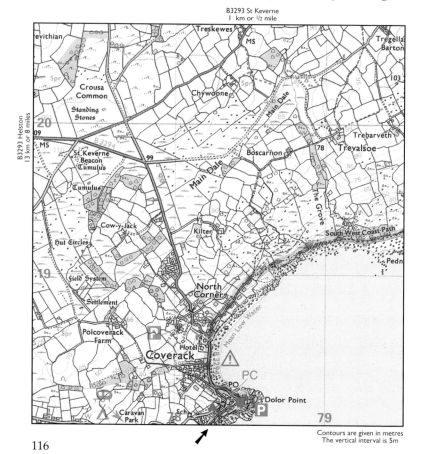

B3293 St Keverne
I km or ½ mile

Contours are given in metres
The vertical interval is 5m

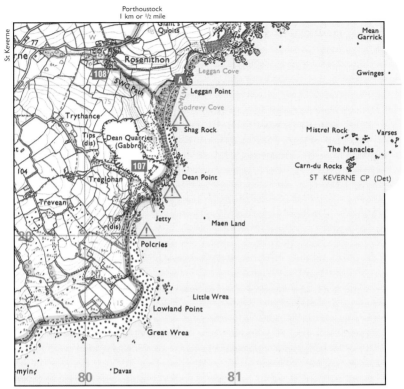

Porthoustock
I km or ¹/₂ mile

Mean
Garrick

Quoits

Rosenithon

108

SWC Path

Leggan Cove

Gwinges

A

Leggan Point

Godrevy Cove

Trythance

Shag Rock

Mistrel Rock

Varses

Tips (dis)

Dean Quarries
(Gabbro)

The Manacles

107

Carn-du Rocks

Treglohan

Dean Point

ST KEVERNE CP (Det)

Trevean

Tips
(dis)

Jetty

Maen Land

Polcries

Little Wrea

Lowland Point

Great Wrea

mying

Davas

80

81

Contours are given in metres
The vertical interval is 5m

interglacial, a warm spell during the Ice Age, the sea is thought to have been higher than at present, because less of the Earth's water would have been in the form of ice. The low, flat ground is a raised beach, now covered with soil and abundant chamomile, and the steep slope is the old cliff. The path now traverses Dean Quarries (Gabbro) **107**, and for your own safety you *must* follow the waymarked route, as it is liable to change when the rock is quarried. Red flags are flown on both the north and the south ends of the site (marked by warning triangles on the map above) and a hooter sounds continuously if blasting is imminent: you must observe these warnings. In 1995 blasting took place 10–10.30 a.m., 1–1.30 p.m., and 5–6.30 p.m.

The offshore rocks due east of the quarry are the notorious Manacles, the scene of many shipwrecks. Probably the best known is the *Mohegan*, which struck at night in a squally southerly wind in 1898 just as the passengers were sitting down to dinner. Over 100 of her passengers and crew are buried in St Keverne churchyard.

117

In 1995 the official route of the Coast Path turned inland **A** at the north end of Godrevy Cove to Rosenithon. Barns in the farmyard **108** are made of rock and cob (mud) with shillet (small pieces of slate). Normally cob walls are plastered and painted over to keep out the wet, so that the composition of the wall is not visible. Cob cottages, the local mud huts, are very comfortable to live in, with superb insulation properties and a large 'thermal mass', so that once the walls are warmed through in winter the temperature of the cottage changes only slowly, while in summer the inside stays cool.

When you reach Porthoustock you can either follow a permissive path along the coast to Porthallow, passing a café at Porthkerris much used by divers – and walkers – or the official route.

On the inland route, on both sides of Porthoustock, care has been taken to make the path follow fields wherever possible, so on the south side the path crosses a hedge **B** into a field just above the former coastguard houses, while on the north the path follows a level track **C** just in front of some cottages. Where the path leaves the road again it follows the side of Porthallow Vineyard **109**, where you can sample the wine and cider for free, and see apple mills and cider presses.

Porthallow (locally known as Pr'alla) village has a bus service, a post office, a café, and a pub called the Five Pilchards, (but neither was serving evening meals in 1995), and a large car park, otherwise called the beach and available at all states of the tide. Just east of the pebbly beach a scramble across the varied rocks provides a wealth of interest for anyone interested in geology. Those whose interest is purely aesthetic will enjoy the contortions of the layers in the wet schist boulders, and the colours of the serpentine.

North of Porthallow, past the intriguingly named Snail's Creep (there is a Cornish dance of the same name), you come to a small headland **110** with access to rich rock pools. From here you can see the narrow raised beach that stretches all the way back to Porthallow. The rocks here form the boundary between the exotic rocks of the Lizard – the schists, gneiss, and serpentine found nowhere else in Cornwall – and the slates, which with the granite make up most of the rest of the county. The boundary is a zone of squeezed-out material – from pebbles to vast boulders – set in slate. Some of the boulders can be seen 50 yards (45 metres) south of the grassy point. Was this part of a gigantic mud and rock slide over 350 million years ago?

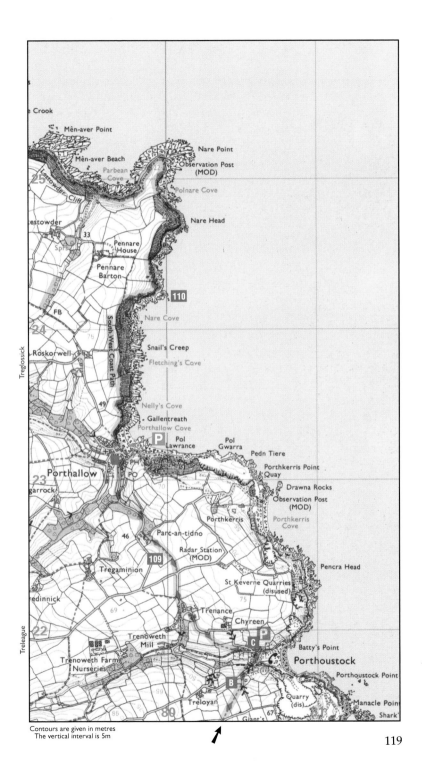

Contours are given in metres
The vertical interval is 5m

119

Dean Quarry provides roadstone for many parts of Britain, and year-round jobs

for about 60 local people.

Nare Head claimed one of the largest four-masted clippers then afloat, the *Bay of Panama*, in a blizzard in March 1891. The ship was carrying jute from Calcutta to Dundee and would have dwarfed the *Cutty Sark*, the tea clipper that is preserved at Greenwich. The wreck was found by a farmer who was looking for his sheep in snowdrifts. He summoned the Coverack Rocket Brigade, who rescued 18 of the crew by breeches buoy.

Gillan Creek can be crossed dry shod, by rather slippery stepping stones **E**, for about one hour before and after low water. The stones are upstream of the grassy banks that narrow the creek appreciably. If this crossing is not possible, the boat-hire firm run a water-taxi and are used to being hailed by walkers. Alternatively you will need to backtrack and follow the directions on the nearby information board **D**, walking up through Flushing towards Manaccan, from where you might wish to go directly to Helford rather than walk along the road on the north side of the creek. St Anthony-in-Meneage occupies what was probably one of the earliest Christian sites in Cornwall. Meneage (pronounced Menayg or Meneeg), 'land of monks', is mentioned in the 10th century.

Just above the church the Coast Path goes through a gate **F** to

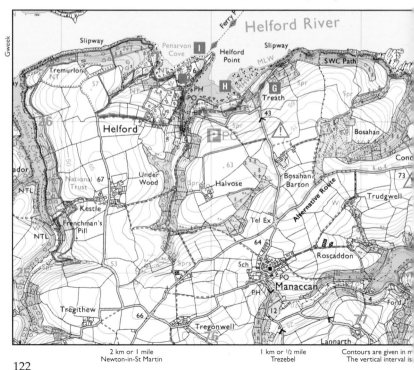

2 km or 1 mile
Newton-in-St Martin

1 km or ¹/2 mile
Trezebel

Contours are given in m
The vertical interval is

enter the Bosahan Estate, which bans dogs, so anyone accompanied by a dog must use the alternative route, by road, to Treath **G**. If dogless, you may enter the estate, and it is worth going on to Dennis Head, where there is not only a prehistoric earthwork but also a square Royalist fortification **111** with gun emplacements at the corners.

Just beyond the junction **G** at Treath the path follows the tarmac road and appears to be heading for the shore, so it is easy to miss the narrow track heading off behind Treath Cottage **H**. You should follow this track, which passes Helford's main car park, before entering the part of the village where all cars (apart from the residents' own) are banned. A stroll along the road past the post office and purveyors of cream teas brings you to the pub, the Shipwright's Arms, and then along a drive to the ferry **I**. A group can summon the ferryman by swinging open the semicircular black board to make a brightly coloured circle, or by using the mobile phone. The normal service is hourly. For details see page 134.

The inlets off the Helford River include Frenchman's Creek, which gave its name to Daphne du Maurier's novel, and Porthnavas Creek, home of the oyster beds and also mussels and clams. Nearby Gweek was a major port in medieval and later times, from which tin was exported. In the past the river was also infamous for an infestation of pirates.

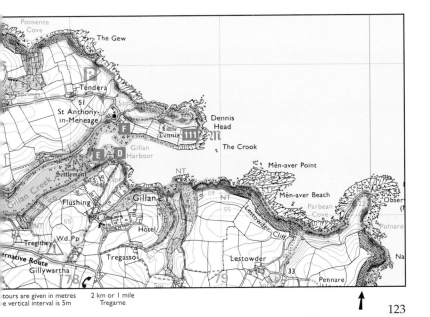

tours are given in metres   2 km or 1 mile
e vertical interval is 5m   Tregarne

123

Once you have crossed the Helford River, the final stage is a gentle walk to Falmouth. The Coast Path follows the road in front of Helford Passage, then goes along the back of the beach into the fields, and passes the gardens of Trebah Manor, famous for Asian and Australian plants. It then enters Durgan village, at the foot of Glendurgan, a sheltered garden full of camellias and azaleas, and also a laurel maze, owned by the National Trust. If the garden is open you can pay the entry fee at the top gate. The path is easy walking through fields past Mawnan, with much bare soil beneath the holm oaks, Rosemullion Head and Gatamala Cove, named after a wreck, to Maenporth ('stony landing-place'). At Mawnan the church tower is used as a landmark to keep sailors clear of the dreaded Manacles: there was even a proposal to paint it white.

There are public conveniences at Maenporth. The path on either side of the cove goes through an exuberance of old man's beard, the wild clematis. In a tiny cove **112** lies the wreck of the *Ben Asdale*, an Aberdeen trawler

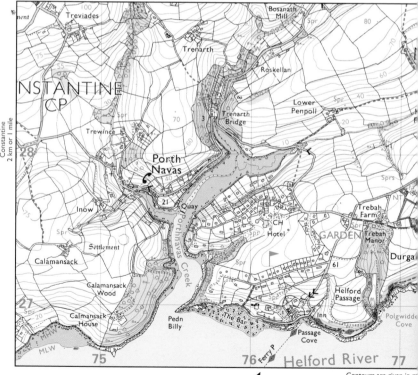

Contours are given in m
The vertical interval is

that went ashore in a gale in December 1978. Her main winch came from the *Conqueror* wrecked near Mousehole in 1977. In the 1970s large shoals of mackerel were coming close inshore in winter, attracting trawlers from all over Europe, with much of the catch being sold for fishmeal, direct to Eastern European and Russian factory ships anchored in Falmouth Bay. Eventually a quota system was introduced which produced the situation that when boats netted a big shoal they would dump a catch that was under the quota. Today not only the pilchards but also the mackerel are gone.

Boslowick
2 km or 1 mile

FALMOUTH BAY

ours are given in metres
e vertical interval is 5m

At Pennance Point **113**, with its monument to Falmouth's Home Guard, is the end of the flue from the old arsenic refinery **114**, built on the site of a lead smelter.

The Coast Path joins the tarmac highway about 90 yards (80 metres) from the café above the south end of Swanpool Beach. Swanpool (probably 'swamp-pool' rather than the more graceful connotation) was the site of a lead-silver mine that was active in the 18th century and finally closed in 1860.

The Coast Path continues along Cliff Road and Castle Drive around Pendennis Point. If you wish to visit Pendennis Castle the entrance is up the hill from the road junction **J**.

The name Pendennis, 'headland of a fort', implies an Iron Age promontory-fort, but only more modern defences are now visible here. South of Crab Quay is a small Tudor blockhouse, Little Dennis, which originally had four guns at ground level. Pendennis Castle was built in 1540–43 as one of a chain stretching from Hull to Milford Haven, for defence against an expected combined fleet from the Pope, Emperor Charles I of Spain, and the King of France. This unlikely alliance of erstwhile enemies was brought about by Henry VIII's Dissolution of the monasteries, his declaration of himself as head of the Church, and his attempts to rid himself of his first wife, Catherine of Aragon (Charles's aunt). That accounted for the Pope and the Emperor: the French joined in because they were the traditional enemy of England anyway!

The massive star-shaped defences around the castle were

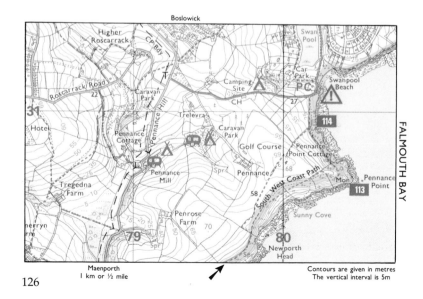

Maenporth
1 km or ½ mile

Contours are given in metres
The vertical interval is 5m

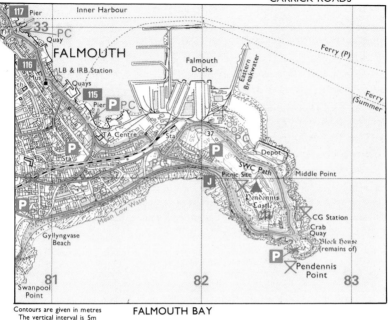

Contours are given in metres
The vertical interval is 5m

FALMOUTH BAY

built by Elizabeth I, and the whole complex's finest hour came with its five-month defence against fellow-countrymen during the Civil War. At the end, the starving Royalist garrison was allowed to march out with full military honours. Victorian modifications included gun emplacements and a barracks, which now houses the youth hostel. People staying at the hostel can visit the castle free between 5 and 6 p.m.

South of the castle on the map lies the 'CG Station' or, more properly, the 'Falmouth Maritime Rescue Co-ordination Centre', whose area extends from the Cornwall/Devon border on the north coast to Dodman Point on the south, and out to 30°W, halfway across the Atlantic. The centre also acts as Britain's link with all 132 other nations in the international maritime rescue system. The centre is open to the public except in July and August: write to HMCG, Falmouth MRCC, Pendennis, Falmouth, TR11 4WZ, suggesting several dates.

Castle Drive continues high above the docks, which specialise in ship repair, and passes Falmouth Docks railway station, from where there are frequent services to Truro. Anchored in Carrick Roads you will sometimes see a large ocean-going tug, ready to dash to any ship in trouble, for a negotiable fee.

The path now follows Bar Road under the railway bridge, then Arwenack Street, Church Street and Market Street, to the Prince of Wales Pier and ferry to St Mawes. Within a few yards of this direct route is a wealth of Falmouth's relatively short history, beginning with Arwenack House, the former manor house of the Killigrew family who planned Falmouth; the Killigrew pyramid, built to beautify the harbour; the Custom House **115** and the Pipe to burn contraband tobacco; the Maritime Museum **116**, and the parish church of King Charles the Martyr. The shore-based Maritime Museum is squeezed into Bell's Court, up an alley opposite Marks & Spencer, and is worth visiting. From the Prince of Wales Pier on Albert Quay **117** the ferry leaves for St Mawes. Details of how to get there and on to Place will be found on page 136; and the Coast Path continues from Falmouth to Exmouth, as described in National Trail Guide no. 10.

Falmouth

The growth of Falmouth from two small fishing villages, Smithick and Pennycomequick, into a major port eclipsing the far older ports of Penryn and Truro, was the work of the Killigrews, a family of whom it could well be said that they had their bread buttered on both sides. One of them spent time in the Fleet Prison, London, for piracy, and then later on became the first governor of Pendennis Castle. His son, also a temporary inhabitant of the Fleet, was Chairman of the Commission of Piracy in Cornwall and thus in charge of prosecuting pirates. This proved fortunate for his wife, who led a gang to plunder a Spanish ship in the harbour and murder the crew; her accomplices were hanged. The grandson continued the entrepreneurial spirit by building the first Lizard lighthouse in 1619 as a money-making venture, but when he had trouble collecting the dues the light went out, much to the wreckers' benefit.

Cornwall and communications

As well as the themes of farming, fishing and mining running as threads through Cornwall's history the county has had a disparate importance in the history of communications.

In Roman times historians were writing about Belerion and Ictis, which some suggest was St Michael's Mount, and implying that trade was long standing. Later a multitude of celtic missionaries from Ireland and Wales came to Cornwall, and some like Wynwallow went on to Brittany. These monks, the

Cornish saints, set up their chapels by the springs which are now venerated as holy wells. Medieval coastal chapels, usually dedicated to St Nicholas, had the safety of seafarers as one of their concerns and showed a light in a window. In time lighthouses were built, and as trade grew, and losses through shipwrecks mounted, further lights filled in the gaps and were built with great difficulty on isolated rocks. Ships which avoided the hazards were guided in by local pilots. Pilot gigs are now enjoying a resurgence as a focus of rivalry between coastal villages like Cadgwith, Porthleven and Padstow, but in the past there were no prizes, and more importantly no pay, for the crew who were runners-up and carried the second pilot to reach the ship.

Falmouth, the most south westerly safe anchorage in Britain was the base for the packet boats – fast, armed ships carrying high-value goods for the Post Office – and also the place where ships called in for orders about where to discharge their cargoes for the best prices. Later Lloyds Signal Station was built on Bass Point and communications between owners and captains became quicker. The Lizard remained the last point for sending messages to outbound ships of the Royal Navy: signallers using semaphore would have been based on hill-tops used by signal beacons dating back to long before the Armada.

The growth of submarine telegraphy speeded communications still further. Cables with copper conductors were brought ashore at Porthcurno, Sennen and Kennack. Marconi's experiments with wireless had a major success when his signal ··· ··· ··· ··· from Poldhu was heard at St John's, Newfoundland in 1901. Intense competition between Marconi's company and the Eastern Telegraph Co. led to an amalgamation as Cable and Wireless, forced by the government who wished both media to prosper. Recent progress in telecommunications in Cornwall has been centred at Goonhilly on Lizard Downs, Britain's first Satellite Earth Station, but in 1995 a new submarine cable, using fibre optics not copper, was brought ashore at Porthcurno.

Falmouth's ship-repair yard has always been well-sited for ships damaged by storms in the Atlantic.

PART THREE

USEFUL
INFORMATION

Transport

Public transport in Cornwall is at its best in summer, but take care if you are told that there is a regular service: regular might mean once a week or term-time only. To help both visitors and residents alike the Cornwall County Council Passenger Transport Unit (at County Hall, Truro, TR1 3AY. Tel: 01872 322142) publishes in early June the *Cornwall Public Transport Timetable*, which is only $1.50 post-free. The main guide has details of all the air, rail, bus and ferry services, but points out that operators can alter services with only six weeks' notice to the Traffic Commissioners. Despite this proviso the guide is vital for anyone walking in Cornwall who may need to use public transport.

Rail

At the time of writing (1999) frequent, regular and fast services connect Plymouth with the rest of Britain and Europe. Many of these services continue at a slower pace into Cornwall, stopping at most of the stations on the main line, which ends at Penzance. Branch lines still connect Newquay, St Ives (change at St Erth or Penzance) and Falmouth (change at Truro) to the main line. Padstow is connected to the main line at Bodmin Parkway station by a Western National bus on Mondays to Saturdays. The major revisions of the railway timetable are made in May and in late September or early October. Information on the current situation should be available by telephoning 0845 7484950.

Buses

Long-distance coach services run by National Express connect Cornwall with the rest of Britain. National Express run direct services to Plymouth, London, Bristol and the North. From Plymouth these National Express services link directly with various places on the Coast Path. For enquiries see National Express in your local phone book. Further links are provided by Western National and a host of smaller operators and connect places on the coast with places inland. These unfortunately do not run along the roads linking coastal villages, apart from a summer service between St Ives and Newquay. Western National sells separate booklets with times of their local services around several towns, but because of the large number of small operators the county council's public transport timetable is more useful.

Ferries

The ferry connecting Padstow and Rock, across the Camel Estuary, runs every day in summer, but not on Sundays from November to March, inclusive. The service is continuous, subject to demand, from 8 a.m., with the last ferry from Rock leaving at 4.50 p.m. in the winter and at 7.50 p.m. in mid-summer, though 'the times of the last ferry are subject to variation with demand'. The ferry is operated by Padstow Harbour Commissioners, Harbour Office, Padstow. Tel. 01841 532239. You are strongly advised to contact the harbour office for up-to-date information, as the land route between Padstow and Rock is long and tortuous, and is ill-served by buses. Apart from the ferry, few boats cross the Camel, so hitching a lift is not a viable option!

The far smaller Gannel Estuary is less of a problem with four bridges, three of which are tidal, and in summer one ferry service. The recommended crossing is over the tidal bridge from the foot of Trethellan Hill, on the northern (Newquay) side, to Penpol Creek, on the southern (Crantock) side. This is not usable for about half an hour (at neaps) to 3 hours (at springs) either side of high water.

The next tidal bridge is near Trenance boating lake and is covered for about half an hour either side of high water but the path across the salt-march on the southern side may be flooded for longer. If you wish to cross the Gannel at high water springs (morning and evening in Cornwall) you will need to use the Trevemper Bridge on the A3075. Finally near the mouth of the Gannel there is a crossing point below the Fern Pit Café which is only available when the café is open, which is daily between 10 a.m. and 6 p.m. from the Spring Bank Holiday to mid-September.

The ferry, tidal bridge and café are all owned and operated by the Northey family, Fern Pit, Riverside Crescent, Newquay, tel. 01637 873181. On the Newquay side the crossing is linked to a private road by a private path through the café's garden and this path is only usable, in either direction, if the café is open. This ferry runs on demand but operations can be curtailed because of adverse sea and weather conditions.

In 1999 there was no ferry service across the Hayle estuary, nor was there any indication that the long-suspended service was about to be reinstated. Hayle Harbour Office, tel. 01736 754043, can provide up-to-date information.

The Helford River has a ferry from Helford Point to Helford Passage which runs between Good Friday and 31 October. The service is hourly, on the hour, between 9 a.m. and 5 p.m. from Helford Passage, with a boat at 6 p.m. in July and August. The return service leaves Helford at 10 minutes past the hour. The service is subject to the weather and tides, but time-tables showing when the tide is too low for the ferry to land should be available in the youth hostels at Falmouth and Coverack, in Helford and Mawnan Smith post offices, and in local pubs (better to enjoy another drink rather than worry about your lack of progress as the tide rises imperceptibly!). The ferry is based at Helford Passage and can be contacted from Helford by the mobile phone or by swinging open the semicircular black board: the ferry will operate on demand for groups. The service is run by Halford River Boats, tel. 01326 250770. The land route is well away from the side of the estuary, is at least 8 miles (13 km) long and mostly on roads.

Between Falmouth and St Mawes there are ferries every day weather permitting. The summer service runs every $\frac{1}{2}$ hour, the winter service every hour. The ferry runs from the Prince of Wales Pier off Albert Quay and times can be obtained from the operator, the St Mawes Ferry Company, tel. 01326 313201.

Between St Mawes and Place there are ferries every day between 1 May and the end of September. Weather permitting, the service runs every half-hour, starting at 10 a.m. from St Mawes, with the return service at 10.15 a.m. from Place, until the last ferry returns from Place at 4.45 p.m. There is no 1 p.m. ferry from St Mawes nor 1.15 p.m. from Place. If required a shuttle service is run, and as the crossing takes 10 minutes each way this can effect the schedules. The service is run by Balcomb Boats, tel. 01209 214901. Between October and April, inclusive, the options are to walk, to catch a bus and walk, or to take a taxi. The shortest route on foot, through St Just and Gerrans, is about 8 miles (13 km) long. Alternatively the harbourmaster or others in St Mawes will put you in touch with a you can contact Western National for details of their service

Information about the four crossing points of the tidal Gannel is provided in the text.

between St Mawes and Portscatho (there were four buses a day in 1999).

Accommodation contacts

The major industry in Cornwall is tourism, so there is an abundance of places to stay: everything from expensive hotels with facilities you probably never dreamed you might need, to spare rooms in farmhouses and meals with the family in the kitchen; also caravan parks, camp sites and youth hostels. But out of season many of the places are shut and in a good season 'No Vacancies' signs are everywhere. The route maps only show caravan and camp sites with the relevant permission from the planning authority; complex planning rules allow other sites to be occupied for a maximum of 28 days per year. Summer visitors will find many of these sites, often with very basic facilities. Sites also set their own rules, which could, for example, mean the minimum stay was two nights, or only family groups were accepted.

The tourist information centres can provide you with lists of places to stay, and for a small fee they will book accommodation at places on their registers. Registered places must meet certain standards, but many excellent B&Bs have not registered, so the fact that the TIC cannot book you a bed in, for example, Zennor does not mean either that there are no B&Bs in the area, or that they are not clean, warm and welcoming. If you are looking for accommodation it makes sense to purchase the annual guide, *The South West Coast Path*, published by the South West Coast Path Association. This lists places to stay, on or near the Coast Path, which welcome walkers. All entries have been recommended by walkers. The main office of the Cornwall Tourist Board is in Daniell Street, Truro, TR1 2DA. Tel. 01872 74057. It is open from 9 a.m. to 5 p.m. Monday to Friday. The West Country Tourist Board also covers Cornwall and has its main office at 60 St David's Hill, Exeter, EX4 4SY. Tel. 01392 425426.

Visitors reaching Cornwall by road will find information about Cornwall in the TICs at Exeter Services on the M5 (Junction 30) and at Marsh Mills Roundabout, near Plymouth, on the A38. Local tourist information centres on or near the Coast Path are listed below.

The Tourist Information Centre, The Red Brick Building, North Quay, Padstow, PL28 8AF. Tel. 01841 533449.

The Tourist Information Centre, Municipal Offices, Marcus Hill, Newquay, TR7 1BD. Tel. 01637 871345.

The Tourist Information Centre, Perranporth, TR6 0DP. Tel. 01872 573368.

The Tourist Information Centre, The Guildhall, Street-an-Pol, St Ives, TR26 2DY. Tel. 01736 796297.

The Tourist Information Centre, Station Approach, Penzance, TR18 2NF. Tel. 01736 62207.

The Tourist Information Centre, 79 Meneage Street, Helston, TR13 8RB. Tel. 01326 565431.

The Tourist Information Centre, 28 Killigrew Street, Falmouth, TR11 3PN. Tel. 01326 312300.

Other contacts

Camping and Caravanning Club, Greenfields House, Westwood Way, Coventry, Warwicks, CV4 8JH. Tel. 0247 669 4995. (Site-list and map available to members.)

Caravan Club, East Grinstead House, East Grinstead, West Sussex, RH19 1UA. Tel. 01342 326944. (Site-list and map available to members.)

Cornwall Outdoors, Cornwall County Council, County Hall, Truro, TR1 3AY. Tel. 01872 322448. (Groups might wish to use the county council's 'outdoor education centres' at Carnyorth north of Land's End, and at St Just-in-Roseland on the east bank of the Fal.)

Landmark Trust, Shottesbrooke, Maidenhead, SL6 3SW. Tel. 01628 825920. (The Egyptian House, Penzance, a cottage at Lower Porthmeor, Zennor and one on Frenchman's Creek on the Helford are available for rent).

National Trust, Cornwall Regional Office, Lanhydrock, Bodmin, Cornwall, PL30 4DE. Tel. 01208 74281. (As well as renting out holiday cottages, the National Trust has lists of its tenants who supply bed and breakfast, and is also assessing the feasibility of converting redundant farm buildings to 'stone-tents', bothy-style overnight stops offering basic accommodation. Groups might be interested in the NT bunkhouse, Beach Head, between Newquay and Treyarnon.)

Ramblers' Association, 1–5 Wandsworth Road, London, SW8 2XX. Tel. 0171 339 8500. Their annual yearbook has many bed and breadfast addresses. Available free to members; available to non-members from major bookshops and newsagents.

South West Coast Path Association (Secretary Eric Wallis), Windlestraw, Penquit, Ermington, Ivybridge, Devon, PL21

OLU. Tel. 01752 896237. (Annual handbook with many useful bed and breakfast addresses, available free to members. Available to non-members from major bookshops and news-agents for £4.99 in 1999).

YMCA, The Orchard, Alverton, Penzance, Cornwall, TR18 4ET. Tel. 01736 65016. (The only residential YMCA centre in this area.)

Youth Hostel Association, English Regional Office, PO Box 11, Matlock, DE4 2XA. (Annual handbook, free to members. Groups might wish to rent a seasonal hotel when it is norm-ally closed.)

Local organisations

You might care to support these groups: they all need funds and members to ensure that the Cornish coastline is both pro-tected and managed to conserve its history and wildlife. If you walk from Padstow to Falmouth you will probably enjoy some of the fruits of their past labours, but they all are active with plans for future work: will you join them?

Carn Brea Mining Society, c/o Camborne School of Mines, Pool, Redruth, TR15 3SE. Tel. 01209 714866.

Cornish Heritage Trust (Membership Secretary, Tony Blackman), 2 The Terrace, Cocks, Perranporth, TR6 0AT. Tel. 01872 572725.

Cornish Maritime Trust (Secretary Gordon Coombs, 47 Hanson Drive, Fowey, PL23 1ET. Tel. 01726 832224. (The Trust con-serves and sails the St Ives lugger *Barnabas*, built in 1881 and the only St Ives mackerel driver in existence, *Softwing*, a Fal-mouth working-boat, and *Ellen*, a Gorran crabber.)

Cornwall Archaeological Society, c/o Royal Institution of Cornwall, River Street, Truro, TR1 2FJ. Tel. 01872 72205.

Cornwall Bird Watching and Preservation Society (Conservation Officer Andy Pay), Salena Cottage, Wendron, Helston, TR13 0EA. Tel. 01326 561628.

Cornwall Wildlife Trust, Five Acres, Allet, Truro, TR4 9DJ. Tel. 01872 273939.

Federation of Old Cornwall Societies (President Joan Rendell, MBE), Tremarsh, Launceston. Tel. 01566 773509.

Groundwork Kerrier, Old Cowlin's Mill, Penhallick, Carn Brea, Redruth, TR15 3YR. Tel. 01209 612917.

St Agnes Museum Trust (Secretary Roger Radcliffe), Kensa, Goonown, St Agnes, TR5 0XD. Tel. 0187255 2181.

South West Coast Path Association, Membership Secretary, 25 Clobells, South Brent, TQ10 9JW. Tel/Fax. 01364 73859. email: coastpath.swcpa@virgin.net. (The association exists to improve the Coast Path, and provides its members with an annual guidebook and newsletters.)

Trevithick Society (Secretary Dr John Ferguson), 15 Abbey Meadow, Lelant, St Ives, TR26 3LL. Tel. 01736 753310.

Trevithick Trust (Chief Executive Stuart Smith), Chygarth, 5 Beacon Terrace, Camborne, TR14 7BU. Tel. 01209 612142.

Other useful addresses

Cornwall Archaeological Unit, Old County Hall, Station Road, Truro, TR1 3AY. Tel. 01872 323603.

Countryside Access Section, Transportation & Estates Department, Cornwall County Council, Castle Canyke Road, Bodmin, Cornwall, PL31 1DZ. Tel. 01872 327850.

Countryside Agency (Headquarters), John Dower House, Crescent Place, Cheltenham, Glos, GL50 3RA. Tel. 01242 521381.

Countryside Agency, South West Regional Office, Bridge House, Sion Place, Clifton, Bristol, BS8 4AS. Tel. 0117 739966.

Countryside Services Section, Planning Department, County Hall, Truro, TR1 3AY. Tel. 01872 322642.

English Nature, Cornwall Office, Trevint House, Strangways Villas, Truro. TR1 2PA. Tel. 01872 262550.

Institute of Cornish Studies, Trevithick Centre, Trevenson Road, Pool, Redruth, TR15 3PL. Tel. 01209 712203.

Lizard Peninsula Countryside Service (Publishes a free annual newspaper, *Lizard & Meneage*, with a diary of events, excellent articles, tide-tables and other information.)

National Trust, Cornwall Regional Office, Lanhydrock, Bodmin, PL30 4DE. Tel. 01208 74281.

North Cornwall Heritage Coast & Countryside Service, Barn Lane, Bodmin, PL31 1LZ. Tel. 01208 893333. (Publishes an annual newspaper, *Coastlines*, which includes a comprehensive programme of guided walks between April and October, plus a countryside calendar twice a year.)

Ordnance Survey, Romsey Road, Maybush, Southampton, SO9 4DH. Tel. 01703 792792.

Royal Society for the Protection of Birds, South West Regional Office, Keble House, Southernhay Gardens, Exeter, EX1 1NT. Tel. 01392 432961.

Hayle-Newquay Countryside Service, Municipal Offices, Marcus Hill, Newquay, TR7 1AF. Tel. 01637 851889.

Hayle-Gwithian Countryside Service, Tehidy Country Park, Camborne, TR14 0HA. Tel. 01872 322106.

Guided walks

The North Cornwall Heritage Coast and Countryside Service, the county council's countryside rangers, Cornwall Wildlife Trust, Cornwall Bird Watching and Preservation Society, Royal Society for the Protection of Birds, National Trust, Trevithick Society, St Agnes Museum Trust, and Groundwork Kerrier have programmes of short walks, usually lasting a couple of hours and led by local experts. There is a small charge for some of the guided walks, but most are free. Details can be obtained from the organisations concerned, and pamphlets are sometimes available in tourist information centres and libraries. The West Cornwall Footpath Society and local groups of the Ramblers' Association also organise a full programme of walks. Many events are listed on CALL, the database accessible in libraries and other public buildings.

Nearby places of interest

Bodmin – linked to the Coast Path at Padstow by the Camel Trail, along which you can walk, cycle or ride a horse. Bodmin was until recently Cornwall's county town and has a Victorian courthouse, the old county jail, the museum of the Duke of Cornwall's Light Infantry, and the largest parish church in the county.

Camborne/Redruth – historically the main mining centre of Cornwall the joined towns contain a wealth of relics of earlier mining plus South Crofty, the only mine now working. Camborne School of Mines has a geological museum, the Trevithick Trust operates two Cornish beam engines owned by the NT, Groundwork Kerrier has a Mineral Tramways Discovery Centre, and soon King Edward Mine will be open to visitors as well as a gateway centre explaining the story of Cornwall's industrial history.

Chysauster – Romano–British village between St Ives and Penzance.

Fal Estuary – various types of craft can be hired at Mylor and at Falmouth and a pleasure boat runs up to Truro.

Goonhilly – satellite Earth station on the Lizard with a visitors' centre that welcomes children.

Helford Estuary – if you wish to explore Frenchman's Creek, Porth Navas and Gweek the best way is by boat. A variety of sailing and motor boats can be hired at St Anthony-in-Meneage and Helford Passage.

Helston – an old 'coinage' town where tin ingots were assayed and where Flora Day, the ancient feast of Beltane, is celebrated on 8 May with Furry Dances and a mumming play, the Hal-an-Tow. Helston is linked to the Coast Path by footpaths on both sides of The Loe. The Folk Museum is in the Old Butter Market.

Trelowarren – a manor house between Gweek and Goonhilly, with the Lizard Visitor Centre and the permanent exhibition centre of the Cornwall Crafts Association.

Trerice – an Elizabethan manor house near Newquay owned by the National Trust. There is a collection of lawn mowers.

Truro – the administrative centre of Cornwall with some pleasant Georgian terraces, the award-winning new Courts of Justice and an excellent museum, the Royal Cornwall Museum, with notable archaeological, mineralogical and art collections.

Wheal Martyn Museum – the industrial archaeology museum of the china clay industry. Wheal Martyn is at Carthew near St Austell.

Bibliography

Balchin, W. G. V., *The Cornish Landscape* (Hodder & Stoughton, 1983).

Betjeman, J., *Betjeman's Cornwall* (Murray, 1984).

Buckley, J. A., *The Cornish Mining Industry* (Tor Mark, 1988).

Cornwall Archaeological Unit, *Cornwall's Archaeological Heritage* (Twelveheads Press, 1990).

Cross, Tom, *Painting the Warmth of the Sun – St Ives Artists 1939–1975* (Alison Hodge and Lutterworth Press, 1984).

Cross, Tom, *The Shining Sands – Artists in Newlyn and St Ives 1880–1930* (Lutterworth, 1994).

Davidson, Alan, *North Atlantic Seafood* (Macmillan, 1979; Penguin, 1980).

Dines, H. G., *The Metalliferous Mining Region of South-West England* (HMSO, 1956 and 1988).

Embrey, P. G. and Symes, R. F., *Minerals of Cornwall and Devon* (British Museum Natural History and Mineralogical Record Inc., 1987).

Flumm, D. S., *A Guide to the Wildlife of the Hayle Estuary* (Cornwall Litho, 1988).

A welcome sight for visitors, but the many reefs and strong tidal currents around Land's End have brought disaster to countless ships.

Harris, K., *Hevva! Cornish Fishing in the Days of Sail* (Truran, 1983).

Kittridge, Alan, *Cornwall's Maritime Heritage* (Twelveheads Press, 1989).

Lawman, Jean, *A Natural History of the Lizard Peninsula* (Truran and the Institute of Cornish Studies, 1994).

Mabey, Richard, *Food for Free* (Collins, 1972 and 1989).

Macadam, John, *A Geology Guide to North Cornwall*(North Cornwall Heritage Coast & Countryside Service,1995).

National Trust Coast of Cornwall Series (10 leaflets cover the area between Padstow and Falmouth).

Ordnance Survey, *Leisure Guide, Cornwall* (Ordnance Survey and Automobile Association, 1987 and 1992).

Padel, O.J., *A Popular Dictionary of Cornish Place-Names* (Alison Hodge, 1988).

Penhallurick, R.D., *Birds of the Cornish Coast* (D. Bradford Barton, 1969).

Pevsner, N., and revised by same and Enid Radcliffe, *Cornwall – The Buildings of England* (Penguin, 1951 and 1970).

Rowse, A.L., *A Cornish Anthology* (Macmillan, 1968; Alison Hodge, 1982 and 1990).

Saunders, Andrew, *Exploring England's Heritage: Devon and Cornwall* (HMSO and English Heritage, 1991).

Soulsby, Ian, *A History of Cornwall* (Phillimore, 1986).

Stanier, Peter H., *Cornwall's Literary Heritage* (Twelveheads Press, 1992).

Stanier, Peter H., *Cornwall's Mining Heritage* (Twelveheads Press, 1988).

Tangye, Michael, *Tehidy and the Bassets* (Truran, 1984).

Tarrant, Michael, *Cornwall's Lighthouse Heritage* (Twelveheads Press, 1990).

Thomas, D.M. (ed.), *The Granite Kingdom: Poems of Cornwall* (D. Bradford Barton, 1970).

Weatherhill, Craig, *Cornovia: Ancient Sites of Cornwall & Scilly* (Alison Hodge, 1985).

Woolf, Virginia, *To the Lighthouse* (Hogarth Press, 1927).

Ordnance Survey Maps covering the South West Coast Path (Padstow to Falmouth)

Landranger Maps (1:50 000): 200, 203, 204.

Explorer Maps (1:25 000):
- 102 (Land's End, Penzance & St Ives)
- 103 (The Lizard, Falmouth & Helston)
- 104 (Redruth & St Agnes)
- 106 (Newquay & Padstow)

Motoring Map: Reach the South West Coast Path area using Travelmaster Map 8, 'South West England and South Wales'.